To Betty

Christmas 2016

Love from

Kate . Klaus

x

FAVOURITE
POEMS
OF THE SEA

FAVOURITE
POEMS
OF THE SEA

Poems to celebrate Britain's
martime heritage

Edited by Howard Watson

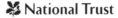
National Trust

First published as *Ode to the Sea* in 2011 by National Trust Books.

This edition first published in the United Kingdom in 2015 by
National Trust Books
1 Gower Street
London WC1E 6HD
An imprint of Pavilion Books Company Ltd

ISBN: 9781909881495

A CIP catalogue record for this book is available from the British Library.

20 19 18 17 16 15
10 9 8 7 6 5 4 3 2

Repro by Mission Productions, Hong Kong
Printed and bound by Toppan Leefung, China

Printed on PREPS (Publishers' Responsible Environmental Paper Sourcing)
compliant paper.

This book can be ordered direct from the publisher at the website:
www.pavilionbooks.com, or try your local bookshop. Also available at
National Trust shops, including www.nationaltrustbooks.co.uk

Contents

Introduction

The British have always had a close relationship with the sea (as islanders must), but it has never been a straightforward one. The sea may have shaped Britain geographically, but it has not defined it politically. Britain has never been a single 'island nation'; indeed, it was not governed by a single parliament until 1707. When James Thomson wrote his famous lines, 'Rule, Britannia, rule the waves; Britons never will be slaves', it was more a hopeful exhortation than a statement of fact. In 1740, when 'Rule Britannia' was first performed in the gardens of Cliveden House in Buckinghamshire, the British Empire and the Royal Navy, on which it depended, were both still relatively modest. As British seamen know better than anyone, no one can 'rule the waves' for long – not least because no one can ever really master the weather. Indeed, the second outdoor performance of 'Rule Britannia' had to be called off, when it started raining.

Yet despite all this, the sea still has a central place in our hearts. When we travel abroad today, it is usually above the waves in an aeroplane or beneath them in a train, but childhood memories of seaside holidays – whether in Cornwall or on the Costas – remain strong. However far we may live from the sea, we still feel its attraction. The founders of the National Trust were no exception. It is not surprising, therefore, that their first acquisition, in 1895, should have been a piece of coastline: Dinas Oleu in Gwynedd, which looks down over Cardigan Bay and out to the Irish Sea beyond. Ever since then, and particularly since the foundation of the Neptune Coastline Campaign in 1965, the National Trust has worked ceaselessly to acquire and conserve beautiful and significant stretches of the British coastline. It now owns over 740 miles of British and Northern Irish coast, including such different places as the White Cliffs of Dover in Kent, the Seven Sisters in East Sussex, the Golden Cap estate in Dorset, the Gower and Llyn peninsulas in Wales, Giant's Causeway in Co. Antrim, Robin Hood's Bay in Yorkshire and Orford Ness in Suffolk.

Like Coleridge's wedding guest in 'The Rime of the Ancient Mariner' (see p.120), we are easily seduced by stories of the sea, and of its heroes and villains.

The National Trust is as much about people as it is about places. So there are few of its properties, however far inland, that do not have some connection with the sea and seamen. At Buckland Abbey in Devon you will find Drake's Drum, celebrated in Sir Henry Newbolt's famous poem (see p.52): when England is threatened, the drum is supposed to beat of its own accord. To Victorian romantics like Newbolt, Francis Drake and the other Elizabethan adventurers such as Richard Grenville, Walter Raleigh and Humphrey Gilbert were unalloyed heroes. Today, we may take a more sober view of their often piratical activities, but the drama of the Spanish Armada's defeat in 1588 still has the power to stir. One Englishman who certainly became a pirate was Sir Francis Verney. After five years spent harassing ships in the eastern Mediterranean he died in wretched circumstances in a Sicilian hospital in 1615. Somehow his splendid purple Turkish robe and slippers found their way back to his home at Claydon in Buckinghamshire. Later in the seventeenth century Admiral George Delaval battled the Barbary pirates of north Africa, accumulating a fortune that he used to save the family estate at Seaton Delaval and to commission a great baroque house from Sir John Vanbrugh. The frieze on the entrance front is decorated with nautical symbols that acknowledge the source of his wealth. The prize money that George Anson earned from capturing a Spanish treasure galleon in 1743 helped to pay for the building of his brother's new house at Shugborough in Staffordshire. Anson went on to lay the foundations of the navy with which Nelson defeated Napoleon. Nelson's flag-captain, 'Kiss Me' Hardy, is commemorated by an obelisk overlooking Weymouth Bay in Dorset.

The British reserve a special place in their affections for circumnavigators such as Drake and Anson. When Francis Chichester achieved this feat single-handed in 1967, he was knighted by the Queen with Drake's sword at Greenwich. A model of the second Sir Francis's boat, Gipsy Moth IV, is displayed in the collection of ship models at Arlington Court in Devon.

The National Trust not only honours the past, but also considers the future of the places in its care. The global problems of rising sea-levels, pollution and coastal erosion demand global solutions, and the National Trust is working with the international community to find them.

Oliver Garnett, The National Trust

2011

Creatures of the Deep

The Maldive Shark

About the Shark, phlegmatical one,
Pale sot of the Maldive sea,
The sleek little pilot-fish, azure and slim,
How alert in attendance be.
From his saw-pit of mouth, from his charnel of maw,
They have nothing of harm to dread,
But liquidly glide on his ghastly flank
Or before his Gorgonian head;
Or lurk in the port of serrated teeth
In white triple tiers of glittering gates,
And there find a haven when peril's abroad,
An asylum in jaws of the Fates!
They are friends; and friendly they guide him to prey,
Yet never partake of the treat–
Eyes and brains to the dotard lethargic and dull,
Pale ravener of horrible meat.

Herman Melville
(1819–1891)

'Tis the Voice
of the Lobster

"'Tis the voice of the Lobster: I heard him declare
"You have baked me too brown, I must sugar my hair."
As a duck with its eyelids, so he with his nose
Trims his belt and his buttons, and turns out his toes.
When the sands are all dry, he is gay as a lark,
And will talk in contemptuous tones of the Shark:
But, when the tide rises and sharks are around,
His voice has a timid and tremulous sound."

"I passed by his garden, and marked, with one eye,
How the Owl and the Panther were sharing a pie:
The Panther took pie-crust, and gravy, and meat,
While the Owl had the dish as its share of the treat.
When the pie was all finished, the Owl, as a boon,
Was kindly permitted to pocket the spoon:
While the Panther received knife and fork with a growl,
And concluded the banquet by–

Lewis Carroll
(1832–1898)

The Smile of the Walrus

The Smile of the Walrus is wide and distraught,
And tinged with pale purples and green,
Like the Smile of a Thinker who thinks a Great Thought,
And isn't quite sure what it means.

Oliver Herford
(1863–1935)

How the Whale Got His Throat

When the cabin port-holes are dark and green
   Because of the seas outside;
   When the ship goes *wop* (with a wiggle between)
And steward falls into the soup-tureen,
   And trunks begin to slide;
When Nursey lies on the floor in a heap,
And Mummy tells you to let her sleep,
   And you aren't waked or washed or dressed,
Why, then you will know (if you haven't guessed)
You're "Fifty North and Forty West!"

Rudyard Kipling
(1865–1936)

A Hymn in Praise of Neptune

Of Neptune's empire let us sing,
At whose command the waves obey;
To whom the rivers tribute pay,
Down the high mountains sliding:
To whom the scaly nation yields
Homage for the crystal fields
  Wherein they dwell:
And every sea-dog pays a gem
Yearly out of his wat'ry cell
To deck great Neptune's diadem.

The Tritons dancing in a ring
Before his palace gates do make
The water with their echoes quake,
Like the great thunder sounding:
The sea-nymphs chant their accents shrill,
And the sirens, taught to kill
  With their sweet voice,
Make ev'ry echoing rock reply
Unto their gentle murmuring noise
The praise of Neptune's empery.

Thomas Campion
(1567–1620)

The Song of the Great Bull Whale

O, I am the Great Bull Whale!
In the storm you shall hear me bellow,
Power bestride of my shoulders, as I tumble the seas aside:
I thrash the deep from ooze to foam, and I churn the froth
all yellow;
For Wa-ha! I am hale–
And when I make sail
My sundering bulk hurls the billows aside
Hurls the billows aside–
Takes a league in a stride,
And slogs, with a bellow, the face of the storm,
'Tis naught when the blood's running warm!

For 'tis naught when the blood's running warm, Wa! Ha!
The might of my bulk in the face of the storm!
  With me! Wa! Ha! Ha!
It has far too much side
For a bit of a breeze on the top of the tide!

For I am the Great Bull Whale!
I smite the sea with my tail–
At the thundering sound the oceans resound
And the Albicore tumbles into a swound
For Wa-ha! I am hale,
And when I make sail
My thundering bulk roars over the tides,
Roars over the tides,
And everything hides,
Save the Albicore-fool! a-splitting his sides–
A fish-kangeroo a-jumping the tides.

For he's naught but a fish and a half, Wa! Ha!
A haddock far less than a young bull calf!
  With me! Wa! Ha! Ha!
He has far too much side
For a bit of haddock a-jump in the tide!

Yes, I am the Great Bull Whale!
I have shattered the moon when asleep
On the face of the deep, by a stroke of my sweep
I have shattered its features pale.
Like the voice of a wandering gale
Is the smite of my sounding tail,
For Wa-ha! I am hale,
And when I make sail
My thundering bulk roars over the tide,
Roars over the tide,
And scatters it wide,
And laughs at the moon afloat on its side–
'Tis naught but a star that has died!

For 'tis naught but a star that had died, Wa! Ha!
A matter of cinders afloat in the Wide!
  With me Wa! Ha! Ha!
It has far too much side
For a cinder afloat in the tide!

William Hope Hodgson
(1877–1918)

The Chambered Nautilus

This is the ship of pearl, which, poets feign
    Sails the unshadowed main,–
    The venturous bark that flings
On the sweet summer wind its purpled wings
In gulfs enchanted, where the siren sings,
    And coral reefs lie bare,
Where the cold sea-maids rise to sun their streaming hair.

Its web of living gauze no more unfurl;
    Wrecked is the ship of pearl!
    And every chambered cell,
Where its dim dreaming life was wont to dwell,
As the frail tenant shaped his growing shell,
    Before thee lies revealed,–
Its irised ceiling rent, its sunless crypt unsealed!

Year after year beheld the silent toil
    That spread his lustrous coil;
    Still, as the spiral grew,
He left the past's year dwelling for the new,
Stole with soft step its shining archway through,
    Built up its idle door,
Stretched in his last-found home, and knew the old no more.

Thanks for the heavenly message brought by thee,
    Child of the wandering sea,
    Cast from her lap, forlorn!
From thy dead lips a clearer note is born
Than ever Triton blew from wreathèd horn!
    While on mine ear it rings,
Through the deep caves of thought I hear a voice
that sings:–

Build thee more stately mansions, O my soul,
    As the swift seasons roll!
    Leave thy low-vaulted past!
Let each new temple, nobler than the last,
Shut thee from heaven with a dome more vast,
    Till thou at length art free,
Leaving thine outgrown shell by life's unresting sea!

Oliver Wendell Holmes
(1809–1894)

The Charge
of the Swordfish

Now when, beneath the riotous drinking,
The witches found the liquor sinking
So low their ladles couldn't reach it,
The blacksmith with a blazing larynx
Organized a swordfish phalanx
And charged the cauldron plate to breach it.
Back from its copper flanks they fell,
The smith had done his work too well.

A Greek:
   From such a race of myrmidons
   Our heroes and our Marathons.

Fabius Maximus:
   It's but the fury of despair.

A French General:
   Magnifique! Mais ce n'est pas la guerre.

Napoleon:
   By some such wild demonic means
   My astral promise was undone.

Nelson:
   By spirits like to such marines
   Trafalgar and the Nile were won.

Carlyle:

    Full ten feet thick that plate was wrought,
    And yet those swordfish tried to ram it;
    Unthinking fools! I never thought
    The sea so full of numskulls, dammit!

Satan:

    Now by my hoof, this recipe
    Is worth a million souls to me;
    But lo! what mortal creature there
    Grins, haunched upon the parapet,
    Whose fierce, indomitable stare
    I long have dreamed of, but not met?

Maryan:

    Most sovereign and most sulphurous lord!
    We, with the help of Cretans, made
    This circumambient palisade
    Of this great height and strength, to ward
    Off such invaders as might mar
    Our feast, and then as sentinel –
    Chief vigilante out of hell –
    We stationed HIM from Zanzibar.

Satan:

    Good! From such audacious seed
    Sprang Heaven's finest, fallen breed,
    Maryan! Ardath! Lulu!
    Try out upon this cat, the brew.

Edwin John Pratt
(1883–1964)

Dolphin

My Dolphin, you only guide me by surprise,
a captive as Racine, the man of craft,
drawn through his maze of iron composition
by the incomparable wandering voice of Phèdre.
When I was troubled in mind, you made for my body
caught in its hangman's-knot of sinking lines,
the glassy bowing and scraping of my will. ...
I have sat and listened to too many
words of the collaborating muse,
and plotted perhaps too freely with my life,
not avoiding injury to others,
not avoiding injury to myself—
to ask compassion... this book, half fiction,
an eelnet made by man for the eel fighting
my eyes have seen what my hand did.

Robert Lowell
(1917–1977)

Coral

This coral's shape echoes the hand
It hollowed. Its

Immediate absence is heavy. As pumice,
As your breast in my cupped palm.

Sea-cold, its nipple rasps like sand,
Its pores, like yours, shone with salt sweat.

Bodies in absence displace their weight,
And your smooth body, like none other,

Creates an exact absence like this stone
Set on a table with a whitening rack

Of souvenirs. It dares my hand
To claim what lovers' hands have never known:

The nature of the body of another.

Derek Walcott
(1930–)

Whales Weep Not!

They say the sea is cold, but the sea contains
the hottest blood of all, and the wildest, the most urgent.

All the whales in the wider deeps, hot are they, as they urge
on and on, and dive beneath the icebergs.
The right whales, the sperm-whales, the hammer-heads, the killers
there they blow, there they blow, hot wild white breath out of the sea!

And they rock, and they rock, through the sensual ageless ages
on the depths of the seven seas,
and through the salt they reel with drunk delight
and in the tropics tremble they with love
and roll with massive, strong desire, like gods.
Then the great bull lies up against his bride
in the blue deep bed of the sea
as mountain pressing on mountain, in the zest of life:
and out of the inward roaring of the inner red ocean of whale blood
the long tip reaches strong, intense, like the maelstrom-tip, and comes to rest
in the clasp and the soft, wild clutch of a she-whale's fathomless body.

And over the bridge of the whale's strong phallus, linking the wonder of whales
the burning archangels under the sea keep passing, back and forth,
keep passing, archangels of bliss
from him to her, from her to him, great Cherubim
that wait on whales in mid-ocean, suspended in the waves of the sea
great heaven of whales in the waters, old hierarchies.

And enormous mother whales lie dreaming suckling their
whale-tender young
and dreaming with strange whale eyes wide open in the waters of
the beginning and the end.

And bull-whales gather their women and whale-calves in a ring
when danger threatens, on the surface of the ceaseless flood
and range themselves like great fierce Seraphim facing the threat,
encircling their huddled monsters of love.
And all this happens in the sea, in the salt
where God is also love, but without words:
and Aphrodite is the wife of whales most happy, happy she!

and Venus among the fishes skips and is a she-dolphin
she is the gay, delighted porpoise sporting with love and the sea
she is the female tunny-fish, round and happy among the males
and dense with happy blood, dark rainbow bliss in the sea.

D.H. Lawrence
(1885–1930)

Jonah

A purple whale
Proudly sweeps his tail
Towards Nineveh;
Glassy green
Surges between
A mile of roaring sea.

"O town of gold,
Of splendour multifold,
Lucre and lust,
Leviathan's eye
Can surely spy
Thy doom of death and dust."

On curving sands
Vengeful Jonah stands.
"Yet forty days,
Then down, down,
Tumbles the town
In flaming ruin ablaze."
 With swift lament

Those Ninevites repent.
They cry in tears,
"Our hearts fail!"
The whale, the whale!
Our sins prick us like spears."

Jonah is vexed;
He cries, "What next? what next?"
And shakes his fist.
"Stupid city,
The shame, the pity,
The glorious crash I've missed."

Away goes Jonah grumbling,
Murmuring and mumbling;
Off ploughs the purple whale,
With disappointed tail.

Robert Graves
(1895–1985)

Sailing on the Seven Seas

Bermudas

Where the remote Bermudas ride
In the ocean's bosome unespied,
From a small boat, that rowed along,
The listening winds received this song.

"What should we do but sing His praise!
That led us through the watery maze,
Unto an Isle so long unknown,
And yet far kinder than our own.
   Where He the huge sea monsters wracks,
That lift the deep upon their backs;
He lands us on a grassy stage,
Safe from the storms, and prelates' rage.
   He gave us this eternal spring,
Which here enamels everything;
And sends the fowls to us in care,
On daily visits through the air.
   He hangs in shades the orange bright,
Like golden lamps in a green night;
And does in the pomegranates close,
Jewels more rich than Ormus show's.
   He makes the figs, our mouths to meet,
And throws the melons at our feet:
But apples, plants of such a price!
No tree could ever bear them twice.
   With cedars, chosen by His hand,

From Lebanon, He stores the land:
And makes the hollow seas, that roar,
Proclaim the ambergris on shore.

  He cast (of which we rather boast)
The gospel's pearl upon our coast:
And in these rocks, for us did frame
A temple, where to sound His name.

  O let our voice His praise exalt,
Till it arrive at heavens vault!
Which thence (perhaps) rebounding, may
Echo beyond the Mexique Bay."

Thus sung they, in the English boat,
An holy and a cheerful note,
And all the way, to guide their chime,
With falling oars they kept the time.

Andrew Marvell
(1621–1678)

Grace Darling

Among the dwellers in the silent fields
The natural heart is touched, and public way
And crowded street resound with ballad strains,
Inspired by one whose very name bespeaks
Favour divine, exalting human love;
Whom, since her birth on bleak Northumbria's coast,
Known unto few but prized as far as known,
A single Act endears to high and low
Through the whole land–to Manhood, moved in spite
Of the world's freezing cares–to generous Youth–
To Infancy, that lisps her praise–to Age
Whose eye reflects it, glistening through a tear
Of tremulous admiration. Such true fame
Awaits her *now*; but, verily, good deeds
Do not imperishable record find
Save in the rolls of heaven, where hers may live
A theme for angels, when they celebrate
The high-souled virtues which forgetful earth
Has witnessed. Oh! that winds and waves could speak
Of things which their united power called forth
From the pure depths of her humanity!
A Maiden gentle, yet, at duty's call,
Firm and unflinching, as the Lighthouse reared
On the Island-rock, her lonely dwelling-place;
Or like the invincible Rock itself that braves,
Age after age, the hostile elements,

As when it guarded holy Cuthbert's cell.
All night the storm had raged, nor ceased, nor paused,
When, as day broke, the Maid, through misty air,
Espies far off a Wreck, amid the surf,
Beating on one of those disastrous isles
Half of a Vessel, half–no more; the rest
Had vanished, swallowed up with all that there
Had for the common safety striven in vain,
Or thither thronged for refuge. With quick glance
Daughter and Sire through optic-glass discern,
Clinging about the remnant of this Ship,
Creatures– how precious in the Maiden's sight!
For whom, belike, the old Man grieves still more
Than for their fellow-sufferers engulfed
Where every parting agony is hushed,
And hope and fear mix not in further strife.
"But courage, Father! let us out to sea–
A few may yet be saved." The Daughter's words,
Her earnest tone, and look beaming with faith,
Dispel the Father's doubts: nor do they lack
The noble-minded Mother's helping hand
To launch the boat; and with her blessing cheered,
And inwardly sustained by silent prayer,
Together they put forth, Father and Child!
Each grasps an oar, and struggling on they go–

Rivals in effort; and, alike intent
Here to elude and there surmount, they watch
The billows lengthening, mutually crossed
And shattered, and re-gathering their might;
As if the tumult, by the Almighty's will
Were, in the conscious sea, roused and prolonged
That woman's fortitude– so tried, so proved–
May brighten more and more!
True to the mark,
They stem the current of that perilous gorge,
Their arms still strengthening with the strengthening heart,
Though danger, as the Wreck is neared, becomes
More imminent. Not unseen do they approach;
And rapture, with varieties of fear
Incessantly conflicting, thrills the frames
Of those who, in that dauntless energy,
Foretaste deliverance; but the least perturbed
Can scarcely trust his eyes, when he perceives
That of the pair– tossed on the waves to bring
Hope to the hopeless, to the dying, life–
One is a Woman, a poor earthly sister,
Or, be the Visitant other than she seems,
A guardian Spirit sent from pitying Heaven,
In woman's shape. But why prolong the tale,
Casting weak words amid a host of thoughts

Armed to repel them? Every hazard faced
And difficulty mastered, with resolve
That no one breathing should be left to perish,
This last remainder of the crew are all
Placed in the little boat, then o'er the deep
Are safely borne, landed upon the beach,
And, in fulfilment of God's mercy, lodged
Within the sheltering Lighthouse.–Shout, ye Waves
Send forth a song of triumph. Waves and Winds,
Exult in this deliverance wrought through faith
In Him whose Providence your rage hath served!
Ye screaming Sea-mews, in the concert join!
And would that some immortal Voice–a Voice
Fitly attuned to all that gratitude
Breathes out from floor or couch, through pallid lips
Of the survivors–to the clouds might bear–
Blended with praise of that parental love,
Beneath whose watchful eye the Maiden grew
Pious and pure, modest and yet so brave,
Though young so wise, though meek so resolute–
Might carry to the clouds and to the stars,
Yea, to celestial Choirs, GRACE DARLING'S name!

William Wordsworth
(1770–1850)

Song from *The Tempest*

The Master, the Swabber, the Boat-swain and I;
The Gunner, and his Mate,
Lov'd Mall, Meg and Marian, and Margery,
But none of us car'd for Kate,
For she had a tongue with a tang,
Would cry to a Sailour go hang:
She lov'd not the savour of Tar nor of Pitch,
Yet a Taylor might scratch her where ere she did itch.
Then to Sea Boys, and let her go hang.

William Shakespeare
(1564–1616)

Anchors

In a breaker's yard by the Millwall Docks,
With its piled-up litter of sheaveless blocks,
Stranded hawsers and links of cable,
A cabin lamp and a chartroom table,
Nail-sick timbers and heaps of metal
Rusty and red as an old tin kettle,
Scraps that were ships in the years gone by,
Fluke upon stock the anchors lie.

Every sort of a make of anchor
For trawler or tugboat, tramp or tanker,
Anchors little and anchors big
For every build and for every rig,
Old wooden-stocked ones fit for the Ark,
Stockless and squat ones, ugly and stark,
Anchors heavy and anchors small,
Mushroom and grapnel and kedge and all.

Mouldy old mudhooks, there they lie!
Have they ever a dream as the days go by
Of the tug of the tides on coasts afar,
A Northern light and a Southern star,
The mud and sand of a score of seas,
And the chuckling ebb of a hundred quays,
The harbour sights and the harbour smells,
The swarming junks and the temple bells?

Roar of the surf on coral beaches,
Rose-red sunsets on landlocked reaches,
Strange gay fishes in cool lagoons,
And palm-thatched cities in tropic noons;
Song of the pine and sigh of the palm,
River and roadstead, storm and calm—

Do they dream of them all now their work is done,
And the neaps and the springs at the last are one?

And only the tides of London flow,
Restless and ceaseless, to and fro;
Only the traffic's rush and roar
Seems a breaking wave on a far-off shore,
And the wind that wanders the sheds among
The ghost of an old-time anchor song:—

> *"Bright plates and pannikins*
> *To sail the seas around,*
> *And a new donkey's breakfast*
> *For the outward bound!"*

Cicely Fox Smith
(1882–1954)

One Who Knows His Sea-gulls

Two sea-gulls carved of ivory
Stand by the early morning-sea.

One has a head, and one has none,
His clean white breast-feathers run
Up and over and do not stop,
There is no sign of that large drop
Of dark fire, round as sky,
That could be called a sea-gull's eye.

Yet one who knows his sea-gulls knows
There is a head hid in the snows
Of the feathers on the back
Of the headless one, and black
Beads of life are sheathed there sound,
Ready to build a world around
The circle of a sea-gull's head
At the lightest alien tread.

A sea-gull's beak is made to slide
Between his wings in back and hide,
His head is made exactly right
To go between his wings for night.

Robert P. Tristram Coffin
(1892–1955)

Horses on the Camargue

In the grey wastes of dread,
The haunt of shattered gulls where nothing moves
But in a shroud of silence like the dead,
I heard a sudden harmony of hooves,
And, turning, saw afar
A hundred snowy horses unconfined,
The silver runaways of Neptune's car
Racing, spray-curled, like waves before the wind.
Sons of the Mistral, fleet
As him with whose strong gusts they love to flee,
Who shod the flying thunders on their feet
And plumed them with the snortings of the sea;
Theirs is no earthly breed
Who only haunts the verges of the earth
And only on the sea's salt herbage feed–
Surely the great white breakers gave them birth.
For when for years a slave,
A horse of the Camargue, in alien lands,
Should catch some far-off fragrance of the wave
Carried far inland from this native sands,
Many have told the tale
Of how in fury, foaming at the rein,
He hurls his rider; and with lifted tail,
With coal-red eyes and catarcating mane,
Heading his course for home,
Though sixty foreign leagues before him sweep,
Will never rest until he breathes the foam
And hears the native thunder of the deep.
And when the great gusts rise
And lash their anger on these arid coasts,
When the scared gulls career with mournful cries

And whirl across the waste like driven ghosts;
When hail and fire converge,
The only souls to which they strike no pain
Are the white-crested fillies of the surge
And the white horses of the windy plain.
Then in their strength and pride
The stallions of the wilderness rejoice;
They feel their Master's trident in their side,
And high and shrill they answer to his voice.
With white tails smoking free,
Long streaming manes, and arching necks, they show
Their kinship to their sisters of the sea–
And forward hurl their thunderbolts of snow.
Still out of hardship bred,
Spirits of power and beauty and delight
Have ever on such frugal pasture fed
And loved to course with tempests through the night.

Roy Campbell
(1902–1957)

In Romney Marsh

As I went down to Dymchurch Wall,
   I heard the South sing o'er the land
I saw the yellow sunlight fall
   On knolls where Norman churches stand.

And ringing shrilly, taut and lithe,
   Within the wind a core of sound,
The wire from Romney town to Hythe
   Along its airy journey wound.

A veil of purple vapour flowed
   And trailed its fringe along the Straits;
The upper air like sapphire glowed:
   And roses filled Heaven's central gates.

Masts in the offing wagged their tops;
   The swinging waves pealed on the shore;
The saffron beach, all diamond drops
   And beads of surge, prolonged the roar.

As I came up from Dymchurch Wall,
  I saw above the Downs' low crest
The crimson brands of sunset fall,
  Flicker and fade from out the West.

Night sank: like flakes of silver fire
  The stars in one great shower came down;
Shrill blew the wind; and shrill the wire
  Rang out from Hythe to Romney town.

The darkly shining salt sea drops
  Streamed as the waves clashed on the shore;
The beach, with all its organ stops
  Pealing again, prolonged the roar.

John Davidson
(1857–1909)

How lovely is the sound of oars at night
And unknown voices, borne through windless air,
From shadowy vessels floating out of sight
Beyond the harbour lantern's broken glare
To those piled rocks that make on the dark wave
Only a darker stain. The splashing oars
Slide softly on as in an echoing cave
And with the whisper of the unseen shores
Mingle their music, till the bell of night
Murmurs reverberations low and deep
That droop towards the land in swooning flight
Like whispers from the lazy lips of sleep.
The oars grow faint. Below the cloud-dim hill
The shadows fade and now the bay is still.

Edward Shanks
(1892–1953)

The Old Ships

I have seen the old ships sail like swans asleep
Beyond the village which men still call Tyre,
With leaden age o'ercargoed, dipping deep
For Famagusta and the hidden sun
That rings black Cyprus with a lake of fire;
And all those ships were certainly so old–
Who knows how oft with squat and noisy gun,
Questing brown slaves or Syrian oranges,
The pirate Genoese
Hell-raked them till they rolled
Blood, water, fruit and corpses up the hold.
But now through friendly seas they softly run,
Painted the mid-sea blue or shore-sea green,
Still patterned with the vine and grapes in gold.
But I have seen,

Pointing her shapely shadows from the dawn
And image tumbled on a rose-swept bay,
A drowsy ship of some yet older day;
And, wonder's breath indrawn,
Thought I–who knows–who knows–but in that same
(Fished up beyond Aeaea, patched up new
–Stern painted brighter blue–)
That talkative, bald-headed pirate came
(Twelve patient comrades sweating at the oar)
From Troy's doom-crimson shore,
And with great lies about his wooden horse
Set the crew laughing, and forgot his course.

It was so old a ship–who knows, who knows?
–And yet so beautiful, I watched in vain
To see the mast burst open with a rose,
And the whole deck put on its leaves again.

James Elroy Flecker
(1884–1915)

Port of Holy Peter

The blue lagoon rocks and quivers,
    Dull gurgling eddies twist and spin,
The climate does for people's livers,
     It's a nasty place to anchor in
        Is Spanish port,
        Fever port,
        Port of Holy Peter.

The town begins on the sea-beaches,
    And the town's mad with stinging flies,
The drinking water's mostly leeches,
     It's a far remove from Paradise
        Is Spanish port,
        Fever port,
        Port of Holy Peter.

There's sand-bagging and throat-slitting,
    And quiet graves in the sea slime,
Stabbing, of course, and rum-hitting,
     Dirt, and drink, and stink, and crime,
        Is Spanish port,
        Fever port,
        Port of Holy Peter.

All the day the wind's blowing
    From the sick swamp below the hills,
All the night the plague's growing,
    And the dawn brings the fever chills
        Is Spanish port,
        Fever port,
        Port of Holy Peter.

You get a thirst there's no slaking,
    You get the chills and fever-shakes,
Tongue yellow and head aching,
    And then the sleep that never wakes.
And all the year the heat's baking,
    The sea rots and the earth quakes,
        Is Spanish port,
        Fever port,
        Port of Holy Peter.

John Masefield
(1878–1967)

At the Sea-Side

When I was down beside the sea
A wooden spade they gave to me
To dig the sandy shore.

My holes were empty like a cup.
In every hole the sea came up,
Till it could come no more.

Robert Louis Stevenson
(1850–1894)

Drake's Drum

Drake he's in his hammock an' a thousand miles away,
  (Capten, art tha sleepin' there below?)
Slung atween the round shot in Nombre Dios Bay,
  An' dreamin' arl the time O' Plymouth Hoe.
Yarnder lumes the Island, yarnder lie the ships,
  Wi' sailor lads a-dancing' heel-an'-toe,
An' the shore-lights flashin', an' the night-tide dashin',
  He sees et arl so plainly as he saw et long ago.

Drake he was a Devon man, an' ruled the Devon seas,
  (Capten, art tha' sleepin' there below?)
Roving' tho' his death fell, he went wi' heart at ease,
  A' dreamin' arl the time o' Plymouth Hoe.
"Take my drum to England, hang et by the shore,
  Strike et when your powder's runnin' low;
If the Dons sight Devon, I'll quit the port o' Heaven,
  An' drum them up the Channel as we drummed them long ago."

Drake he's in his hammock till the great Armadas come,
  (Capten, art tha sleepin' there below?)
Slung atween the round shot, listenin' for the drum,
  An' dreamin arl the time o' Plymouth Hoe.
Call him on the deep sea, call him up the Sound,
  Call him when ye sail to meet the foe;
Where the old trade's plyin' an' the old flag flyin'
  They shall find him ware an' wakin', as they found
him long ago!

Sir Henry Newbolt
(1862–1938)

A Ballad to Queen Elizabeth of the Spanish Armada

King Philip had vaunted his claims:
  He had sworn for a year that he would sack us;
With an army of heathenish names
  He was coming to fagot and stack us;
  Like the thieves of the sea he would track us.
And shatter our ships on the main;
  But we had bold Neptune to back us,–
And where are the galleons of Spain?

His carackes were christened of dames
  To the kirtles whereof he would tack us;
With his saints and his gilded stern-frames,
  He had thought like an egg-shell to crack us;
  Now Howard may get to his Flaccus,
And Drake to his Devon again,
  And Hawkins bowl rubbers to Bacchus,–
For where are the galleons of Spain?

Let his Majesty hang to St. James
  The axe that he whetted to axe us;
He must play at some lustier games
  Or at sea he can hope to out-thwack us;
  To his mines of Peru he would pack us
To tug at the bullet and chain;
  Alas! that his Greatness would lack us!–
But where are the galleons of Spain?

Envoy

  Gloriana! the don may attack us
Whenever his stomach may be fain;
  He must reach us before he can rack us,–
And where are the galleons of Spain?

Austin Dobson
(1840–1921)

Greenland Whale Fisheries

In eighteen hundred and forty-five,
Being March on the twentieth day,
Oh, we hoisted our colours to our topmost high
And for Greenland forged away, brave boys
And for Greenland forged away.

When we struck that Greenland shore
With our gallant ship in full fold,
We wished ourselves back safe home again
With our friends all on the shore, brave boys
With our friends all on the shore.
Our mate stood on the forecastle yard
With a spyglass in his hand,
"There's a whale, there's a whale, there's a whale!" cried he,
"And she blows at every span, brave boys,
And she blows at every span."

Oh, when this whale we did harpoon
She made one slap with her tail,
She capsized our boat, we lost five of our crew,
Neither did we catch that whale, brave boys
Neither did we catch that whale.
"Sad news, sad news," to our captain we cried,
Which grieved his heart in full store,
But the losing of five of his jolly, jolly crew,
Oh, it grieved him ten times more, brave boys,
Oh, that grieved him ten times more.

"Hist your anchors then, brave boys," said he.
"Let us leave this cold countery
Where the storm and the snow and the whalefish does blow,
And daylight's seldom seen, brave boys,
And daylight's seldom seen."

Anon.

The Shell

And then I pressed the shell
Close to my ear,
And listened well.

And straightway, like a bell,
Came low and clear
The slow, sad, murmur of far distant seas.

Whipped by an icy breeze
Upon a shore
Wind-swept and desolate.

It was a sunless strand that never bore
The footprints of a man,
Nor felt the weight

Since time began
Of any human quality or stir,
Save what the dreary winds and wave incur.

And in the hush of waters was the sound
Of pebbles, rolling round;
For ever rolling, with a hollow sound:

And, bubbling sea-weeds, as the waters go,
Swish to and fro
Their long cold tentacles of slimy grey:

There was no day;
Nor ever came a night
Setting the stars alight

To wonder at the moon:
Was twilight only, and the frightened croon,
Smitten to whimpers, of the dreary wind

And waves that journeyed blind ...
And then I loosed my ear–Oh, it was sweet
To hear a cart go jolting down the street.

James Stephens
(1882–1950)

Blasted and bored and undermined
    By quarrying seas
Reared the erect chalk-cliff with black flints lined.
    (Flints drop like nuts from trees
When the frost bites
The chalk on winter nights.)

Save for frail shade of jackdaw's flight
    No night was there,
But blue-skyed summer and a cliff so white
    It stood like frozen air;
Foot slipped on damp
Chalk where the limpets camp.

With only purple of sea-stock
    And jackdaw's shade
To mitigate that blazing height of chalk
    I stood like a soul strayed
In paradise
Hiding my blinded eyes.

Andrew Young
(1885–1971)

Dover Beach

The sea is calm tonight.
The tide is full, the moon lies fair
Upon the straits; on the French coast the light
Gleams and is gone; the cliffs of England stand,
Glimmering and vast, out in the tranquil bay.
Come to the window, sweet is the night-air!
Only, from the long line of spray
Where the sea meets the moon-blanched land,
Listen! you hear the grating roar
Of pebbles which the waves draw back, and fling,
At their return, up the high strand,
Begin, and cease, and then again begin,
With tremulous cadence slow, and bring
The eternal note of sadness in.

Sophocles long ago
Heard it on the Aegean, and it brought
Into his mind the turbid ebb and flow
Of human misery; we
Find also in the sound a thought,
Hearing it by this distant northern sea.

The Sea of Faith
Was once, too, at the full, and round earth's shore
Lay like the folds of a bright girdle furled.
But now I only hear
Its melancholy, long, withdrawing roar,
Retreating, to the breath
Of the night-wind, down the vast edges drear
And naked shingles of the world.

Ah, love, let us be true
To one another! for the world, which seems
To lie before us like a land of dreams,
So various, so beautiful, so new,
Hath really neither joy, nor love, nor light,
Nor certitude, nor peace, nor help for pain;
And we are here as on a darkling plain
Swept with confused alarms of struggle and flight,
Where ignorant armies clash by night.

Matthew Arnold
(1822–1888)

Forth from Calais, at dawn of night, when sunset summer on autumn shone,
Fared the steamer alert and loud through seas whence only the sun was gone:
Soft and sweet as the sky they smiled, and bade man welcome: a dim sweet hour
Gleamed and whispered in wind and sea, and heaven was fair as a field
    in flower.
Stars fulfilled the desire of the darkling world as with music: the starbright air
Made the face of the sea, if aught may make the face of the sea, more fair.
Whence came change? Was the sweet night weary of rest? What anguish awoke
    in the dark?
Sudden, sublime, the strong storm spake: we heard the thunders as hounds
that bark.
Lovelier if aught may be lovelier than stars, we saw the lightnings exalt the sky,
Living and lustrous and rapturous as love that is born but to quicken and lighten
    and die.
Heaven's own heart at its highest of delight found utterance in music and
    semblance in fire:
Thunder on thunder exulted, rejoicing to live and to satiate the night's desire.
And the night was alive and an-hungered of life as a tiger from toils cast free:
And a rapture of rage made joyous the spirit and strength of the soul of the sea.
All the weight of the wind bore down on it, freighted with death for fraught:
And the keen waves kindled and quickened as things transfigured or things
    distraught.
And madness fell on them laughing and leaping; and madness came on the wind:
And the might and the light and the darkness of storm were as storm in the heart
    of Ind.
Such glory, such terror, such passion, as lighten and harrow the far fierce East,
Rang, shone, spake, shuddered around us: the night was an altar with death
    for priest.
The channel that sunders England from shores where never was man born free
Was clothed with the likeness and thrilled with the strength and the wrath of a
    tropic sea.
As a wild steed ramps in rebellion, and rears till it swerves from a backward fall,

The strong ship struggled and reared, and her deck was upright as a sheer
 cliff's wall.
Stern and prow plunged under, alternate: a glimpse, a recoil, a breath,
And she sprang as the life in a god made man would spring at the throat of death.
Three glad hours, and it seemed not an hour of supreme and supernal joy,
Filled full with delight that revives in remembrance a sea-bird's heart in a boy.
For the central crest of the night was cloud that thundered and flamed, sublime
As the splendour and song of the soul everlasting that quickens the pulse of time.
The glory beholden of man in a vision, the music of light overheard,
The rapture and radiance of battle, the life that abides in the fire of a word,
In the midmost heaven enkindled, was manifest far on the face of the sea,
And the rage in the roar of the voice of the waters was heard but when heaven
 breathed free.
Far eastward, clear of the covering of cloud, the sky laughed out into light
From the rims of the storm to the sea's dark edge with flames that were
 flowerlike and white.
The leaping and luminous blossoms of live sheet lightning that laugh as
 they fade
From the cloud's black base to the black wave's brim rejoiced in the light
 they made.
Far westward, throned in a silent sky, where life was in lustrous tune,
Shone, sweeter and surer than morning or evening, the steadfast smile of
 the moon.
The limitless heaven that enshrined them was lovelier than dreams may
 behold, and deep
As life or as death, revealed and transfigured, may shine on the soul
 through sleep.
All glories of toil and of triumph and passion and pride that it yearns to know
Bore witness there to the soul of its likeness and kinship, above and below.
The joys of the lightnings, the songs of the thunders, the strong sea's labour
 and rage,
Were tokens and signs of the war that is life and is joy for the soul to wage.

No thought strikes deeper or higher than the heights and the depths that the
  night made bare,
Illimitable, infinite, awful and joyful, alive in the summit of air–
Air stilled and thrilled by the tempest that thundered between its reign and
  the sea's,
Rebellious, rapturous, and transient as faith or as terror that bows men's knees.
No love sees loftier and fairer the form of its godlike vision in dreams
Than the world shone then, when the sky and the sea were as love for a breath's
  length seems–
One utterly, mingled and mastering and mastered and laughing with love
  that subsides
As the glad mad night sank panting and satiate with storm, and released
  the tides.
In the dense mid channel the steam-souled ship hung hovering, assailed
  and withheld
As a soul born royal, if life or if death be against it, is thwarted and quelled.
As the glories of myriads of glow-worms in lustrous grass on a boundless lawn
Were the glories of flames phosphoric that made of the water a light like dawn.
A thousand Phosphors, a thousand Hespers, awoke in the churning sea,
And the swift soft hiss of them living and dying was clear as a tune could be;
As a tune that is played by the fingers of death on the keys of life or of sleep,
Audible alway alive in the storm, too fleet for a dream to keep:
Too fleet, too sweet for a dream to recover and thought to remember awake:
Light subtler and swifter than lightning, that whispers and laughs in the live
  storm's wake,
In the wild bright wake of the storm, in the dense loud heart of the labouring
  hour,
A harvest of stars by the storm's hand reaped, each fair as a star-shaped flower.
And sudden and soft as the passing of sleep is the passing of tempest seemed
When the light and the sound of it sank, and the glory was gone as a dream
  half dreamed.
The glory, the terror, the passion that made of the midnight a miracle, died,
Not slain at a stroke, nor in gradual reluctance abated of power and of pride;
With strong swift subsidence, awful as power that is wearied of power

upon earth,

As a God that were wearied of power upon heaven, and were fain of a new
    God's birth,

The might of the night subsided: the tyranny kindled in darkness fell:

And the sea and the sky put off them the rapture and radiance of heaven and
    of hell.

The waters, heaving and hungering at heart, made way, and were well-nigh fain,

For the ship that had fought them, and wrestled, and revelled in labour, to cease
    from her pain.

And an end was made of it: only remembrance endures of the glad loud strife;

And the sense that a rapture so royal may come not again in the passage of life.

Algernon Charles Swinburne
(1837–1909)

The Revenge –
A Ballad of the Fleet

I

At Flores in the Azores Sir Richard Grenville lay,
And a pinnace, like a flutter'd bird, came flying from far away:
"Spanish ships of war at sea! we have sighted"
Then sware Lord Thomas Howard: 'Fore God I am no coward;
But I cannot meet them here, for my ships are out of gear,
And the half my men are sick. I must fly, but follow quick.
We are six ships of the line; can we fight with fifty-three?"

II

Then spake Sir Richard Grenville: "I know you are no coward;
You fly them for a moment to fight with them again.
But I've ninety men and more that are lying sick ashore.
I should count myself the coward if I left them, my Lord Howard,
To these Inquisition dogs and the devildoms of Spain."

III

So Lord Howard passed away with five ships of war that day,
Till he melted like a cloud in the silent summer heaven;
But Sir Richard bore in hand all his sick men from the land
Very carefully and slow,
Men of Bideford in Devon,
And we laid them on the ballast down below;
For we brought them all aboard,
And they blest him in their pain, that they were not left to Spain,
To the thumbscrew and the stake, for the glory of the Lord.

IV

He had only a hundred seamen to work the ship and to fight,
And he sailed away from Flores till the Spaniard came in sight,
With his huge sea-castles heaving upon the weather bow.
"Shall we fight or shall we fly?
Good Sir Richard, tell us now,
For to fight is but to die!
There'll be little of us left by the time this sun be set.'
And Sir Richard said again: "We be all good English men.
Let us bang these dogs of Seville, the children of the devil,
For I never turn'd my back upon Don or devil yet."

V

Sir Richard spoke and he laugh'd, and we roar'd a hurrah, and so
The little Revenge ran on sheer into the heart of the foe,
With her hundred fighters on deck, and her ninety sick below;
For half of their fleet to the right and half to the left were seen,
And the little Revenge ran on thro' the long sea-lane between.

VI

Thousands of their soldiers looked down from their decks and laugh'd,
Thousands of their seamen made mock at the mad little craft
Running on and on, till delay'd
By their mountain-like San Philip that, of fifteen hundred tons,
And up-shadowing high above us with her yawning tiers of guns,
Took the breath from our sails, and we stay'd.

VII

And while now the great San Philip hung above us like a cloud
Whence the thunderbolt will fall
Long and loud,
Four galleons drew away
From the Spanish fleet that day,
And two upon the larboard and two upon the starboard lay,
And the battle-thunder broke from them all.

VIII

But anon the great San Philip, she bethought herself and went
Having that within her womb that had left her ill content;
And the rest they came aboard us, and they fought us hand to hand,
For a dozen times they came with their pikes and musqueteers,
And a dozen times we shook 'em off as a dog that shakes his ears
When he leaps from the water to the land.

IX

And the sun went down, and the stars came out far over the summer sea,
But never a moment ceased the fight of the one and the fifty-three.
Ship after ship, the whole night long, their high-built galleons came,
Ship after ship, the whole night long, with her battle-thunder and flame;
Ship after ship, the whole night long, drew back with her dead and her shame.
For some were sunk and many were shatter'd, and so could fight us no more–
God of battles, was ever a battle like this in the world before?

X

For he said "Fight on! fight on!"
Tho' his vessel was all but a wreck;
And it chanced that, when half of the short summer night was gone,
With a grisly wound to be dressed he had left the deck,
But a bullet struck him that was dressing it suddenly dead,
And himself he was wounded again in the side and the head,
And he said "Fight on! fight on!"

XI

And the night went down, and the sun smiled out far over the summer sea,
And the Spanish fleet with broken sides lay round us all in a ring;
But they dared not touch us again, for they fear'd that we still could sting,
So they watched what the end would be.
And we had not fought them in vain,
But in perilous plight were we,
Seeing forty of our poor hundred were slain,
And half of the rest of us maim'd for life
In the crash of the cannonades and the desperate strife;
And the sick men down in the hold were most of them stark and cold,
And the pikes were all broken or bent, and the powder was all of it spent;
And the masts and the rigging were lying over the side;
But Sir Richard cried in his English pride,
"We have fought such a fight for a day and a night
As may never be fought again!
We have won great glory, my men!
And a day less or more
At sea or ashore,
We die—does it matter when?
Sink me the ship, Master Gunner—sink her, split her in twain!
Fall into the hands of God, not into the hands of Spain!"

XII

And the gunner said "Ay, ay", but the seamen made reply:
"We have children, we have wives,
And the Lord hath spared our lives.
We will make the Spaniard promise, if we yield, to let us go;
We shall live to fight again and to strike another blow."
And the lion there lay dying, and they yielded to the foe.

XIII

And the stately Spanish men to their flagship bore him then,
Where they laid him by the mast, old Sir Richard caught at last,
And they praised him to his face with their courtly foreign grace;
But he rose upon their decks, and he cried:
"I have fought for Queen and Faith like a valiant man and true;
I have only done my duty as a man is bound to do:
With a joyful spirit I Sir Richard Grenville die!"
And he fell upon their decks, and he died.

XIV

And they stared at the dead that had been so valiant and true,
And had holden the power and glory of Spain so cheap
That he dared her with one little ship and his English few;
Was he devil or man? He was devil for aught they knew,
But they sank his body with honour down into the deep,
And they mann'd the Revenge with a swarthier alien crew,
And away she sail'd with her loss and long'd for her own;
When a wind from the lands they had ruin'd awoke from sleep,
And the water began to heave and the weather to moan,
And or ever that evening ended a great gale blew,
And a wave like the wave that is raised by an earthquake grew,
Till it smote on their hulls and their sails and their masts and their flags,
And the whole sea plunged and fell on the shot-shatter'd navy of Spain,
And the little Revenge herself went down by the island crags
To be lost evermore in the main.

Alfred, Lord Tennyson
(1809–1892)

Casabianca

The boy stood on the burning deck
   Whence all but he had fled;
The flame that lit the battle's wreck
   Shone round him o'er the dead.

Yet beautiful and bright he stood,
   As born to rule the storm;
A creature of heroic blood,
   A proud though childlike form.

The flames roll'd on—he would not go
   Without his father's word;
That father, faint in death below,
   His voice no longer heard.

He call'd aloud, "Say, father, say
   If yet my task is done?"
He knew not that the chieftain lay
   Unconscious of his son.

"Speak, father!" once again he cried
  "If I may yet be gone!"
And but the booming shots replied,
  And fast the flames rolled on.

Upon his brow he felt their breath,
  And in his waving hair;
And looked from that lone post of death,
  In still, yet brave despair;

And shouted but once more aloud,
  "My father! must I stay?"
While o'er him fast, through sail and shroud
  The wreathing fires made way,

They wrapt the ship in splendour wild,
  They caught the flag on high,
And stream'd above the gallant child
  Like banners in the sky.

There came a burst of thunder sound–
  The boy–oh! where was he?
–Ask of the winds that far around
  With fragments strew the sea;

With mast, and helm, and pennon fair,
  That well had borne their part–
But the noblest thing that perished there
  Was that young, faithful heart.

Felicia Dorothea Hemans
(1793–1835)

'Soldier an' Sailor Too'

(The Royal Regiment of Marines)

As I was spittin' into the Ditch aboard o' the Crocodile,
I seed a man on a man-o'-war got up in the Reg'lars' style.
'E was scrapin' the paint from off of 'er plates, an' I sez to 'im, "'Oo are you?"
Sez 'e, "I'm a Jolly–'Er Majesty's Jolly –soldier an' sailor too!"
Now 'is work begins by Gawd knows when, and 'is work is never through;
'E isn't one o' the reg'lar Line, nor 'e isn't one of the crew.
'E's a kind of a giddy harumfrodite–soldier an' sailor too!

An' after I met 'im all over the world, a-doin' all kinds of things,
Like landin' 'isself with a Gatlin' gun to talk to them 'eathen kings;
'E sleeps in an 'ammick instead of a cot, an' 'e drills with the deck on a slew,
An' 'e sweats like a Jolly–'Er Majesty's Jolly–soldier an' sailor too!
For there isn't a job on the top o' the earth the beggar don't know, nor do–
You can leave 'im at night on a bald man's 'ead, to paddle 'is own canoe–
'E's a sort of a bloomin' cosmopolouse–soldier an' sailor too.

We've fought 'em in trooper, we've fought 'em in dock, and drunk with
    'em in betweens,
When they called us the seasick scull'ry-maids, an' we called 'em the
    Ass Marines;
But, when we was down for a double fatigue, from Woolwich to Bernardmyo,
We sent for the Jollies –'Er Majesty's Jollies –soldier an' sailor too!
They think for 'emselves, an' they steal for 'emselves, and they never ask
    what's to do,
But they're camped an' fed an' they're up an' fed before our bugle's blew.
Ho! they ain't no limpin' procrastitutes–soldier an' sailor too.

You may say we are fond of an 'arness-cut, or 'ootin' in barrick-yards,
Or startin' a Board School mutiny along o' the Onion Guards;
But once in a while we can finish in style for the ends of the earth to view,
The same as the Jollies–'Er Majesty's Jollies–soldier an' sailor too!
They come of our lot, they was brothers to us; they was beggars we'd met
   an' knew;
Yes, barrin' an inch in the chest an' the arm, they was doubles o' me an' you;
For they weren't no special chrysanthemums–soldier an' sailor too!

To take your chance in the thick of a rush, with firing all about,
Is nothing so bad when you've cover to 'and, an' leave an' likin' to shout;
But to stand an' be still to the Birken'ead drill is a damn tough bullet to chew,
An' they done it, the Jollies–'Er Majesty's Jollies–soldier an' sailor too!
Their work was done when it 'adn't begun; they was younger nor me an' you;
Their choice it was plain between drownin' in 'eaps an' bein' mopped by
   the screw,
So they stood an' was still to the Birken'ead drill, soldier an' sailor too!

We're most of us liars, we're 'arf of us thieves, an' the rest are as rank as can be,
But once in a while we can finish in style (which I 'ope it won't 'appen to me).
But it makes you think better o' you an' your friends, an' the work you may
   'ave to do,
When you think o' the sinkin' Victorier's Jollies–soldier an' sailor too!
Now there isn't no room for to say ye don't know– they 'ave proved it plain
   and true–
That whether it's Widow, or whether it's ship, Victorier's work is to do,
An' they done it, the Jollies–'Er Majesty's Jollies –soldier an' sailor too!

Rudyard Kipling
(1865—1936)

Homeward Bound

They will take us from the moorings, they will take us from the Bay,
    They will pluck us up to windward when we sail.
We shall hear the keen wind whistle, we shall feel the sting of spray,
    When we've dropped the deep-sea pilot o'er the rail.
Then it's Johnnie heave an' start her, then it's Johnnie roll and go;
    When the mates have picked the watches, there is little rest for Jack.
But we'll raise the good old chanty that the Homeward bounders know,
    For the girls have got the tow-rope, an' they're hauling in the slack

In the dusty streets and dismal, through the noises of the town,
    We can hear the West wind humming through the shrouds;
We can see the lightning leaping when the tropic suns go down,
    And the dapple of the shadows of the clouds.
And the salt blood dances in us, to the tune of Homeward Bound,
    To the call to weary watches, to the sheet and to the tack.
When they bid us man the capstan how the hands will walk her round! –
    For the girls have got the tow-rope, an' they're hauling in the slack.

Through the sunshine of the tropics, round the bleak and dreary Horn,
Half across the little planet lies our way.
We shall leave the land behind us like a welcome that's outworn
When we see the reeling mastheads swing and sway.
Through the weather fair or stormy, in the calm and in the gale,
We shall heave and haul to help her, we shall hold her on her track,
And you'll hear the chorus rolling when the hands are making sail,
For the girls have got the tow-rope, an' they're hauling in the slack!

D.H. Rogers
(unknown)

Stormy Weather

Sea-Fever

I must go down to the seas again, to the lonely sea and the sky,
And all I ask is a tall ship and a star to steer her by,
And the wheel's kick and the wind's song and the white sail's shaking,
And a grey mist on the sea's face and a grey dawn breaking.

I must go down to the seas again, for the call of the running tide
Is a wild call and a clear call that may not be denied;
And all I ask is a windy day with the white clouds flying,
And the flung spray and the blown spume, and the sea-gulls crying.

I must go down to the seas again to the vagrant gypsy life,
To the gull's way and the whale's way where the wind's like
a whetted knife;
And all I ask is a merry yarn from a laughing fellow-rover,
And quiet sleep and a sweet dream when the long trick's over.

John Masefield
(1878–1967)

The Way of the Wind

The wind's way in the deep sky's hollow
None may measure, as none can say
How the heart in her shows the swallow
    The wind's way.

Hope nor fear can avail to stay
Waves that whiten on wrecks that wallow,
Times and seasons that wane and slay.

Life and love, till the strong night swallow
Thought and hope and the red last ray,
Swim the waters of years that follow
    The wind's way.

Algernon Charles Swinburne
(1837–1909)

The Fog-Sea

I

The morning is ten thousand miles away.
The winter night surrounds me, vast and cold,
Without a star. The voiceless fog is rolled
From ocean-levels desolate and grey;
But over all the floods of moonlight lay
A glory on those billows that enfold
The muffled sea and forest. Gaunt and old,
The dripping redwoods wait the distant day.
Unknown, above, what silver-dripping waves
Break slowly on the purple reefs of night!
What radiant foam ascends from shadowy bars,
Or sinks unechoing to soundless caves!
No whisper is upon those tides of light,
Setting in silence toward the risen stars.

II

O phantom sea, pale spirit of unrest!
There is no thunder where your billows break.
Morning shall be your strand; your waters make
An island of the mountain-top, whose crest
Is lonely on the ocean of your breast.
No sail is there save what our visions take
Of mist and moonlight, on whose ghostly wake
Our dreams go forth unuttered to the West.
The splendour on your tides is high and far,
Seen by the mind alone, whose wings can sweep
On wilder glories and a vaster deep.
Chill are your gulfs, O sea without a song!
Hiding the heavens from man, man from the star,
To which your parent sea endures as long.

George Sterling
(1869–1926)

O Come Quickly!

Never weather-beaten sail more willing bent to shore,
Never tirèd pilgrim's limbs affected slumber more,
Than my wearied sprite now longs to fly out of my troubled breast:
O come quickly, sweetest Lord, and take my soul to rest!

Ever blooming are the joys of heaven's high Paradise,
Cold age deafs not there our ears nor vapour dims our eyes:
Glory there the sun outshines; whose beams the Blessèd only see:
O come quickly, glorious Lord, and raise my sprite to Thee!

Thomas Campion
(1567–1620)

Deep-Sea Calm

With what deep calm, and passionlessly great,
Thy central soul is stored, the Equinox
Roars, and the North Wind drives ashore his flocks,
Thou heedest not, thou dost not feel the weight
Of the Leviathan, the ships in state
Plough on, and hull with hull in battle shocks,
Unshaken thou; the trembling planet rocks,
Yet thy deep heart will scarcely palpitate.
Peace-girdle of the world, thy face is moved,
And now thy furrowed brow with fierce light gleams,
Now laughter ripples forth a thousand miles,
But still the calm of thine abysmal streams
Flows round the people of our fretful isles,
And Earth's inconstant fever is reproved.

H.D. Rawnsley
(1851–1920)

The Open Sea

From my window I can see,
Where the sandhills dip,
One far glimpse of open sea.
Just a slender slip
Curving like a crescent moon–
Yet a greater prize
Than the harbour garden-fair
Spread beneath my eyes.

Just below me swings the bay,
Sings a sunny tune,
But my heart is far away
Out beyond the dune;
Clearer far the sea-gulls' cry
And the breakers' roar,
Than the little waves beneath
Lapping on the shore.

For that strip of sapphire sea
Set against the sky
Far horizons means to me–
And the ships go by
Framed between the empty sky
And the yellow sands,
While my freed thoughts follow them
Out to other lands.

All its changes who can tell?
I have seen it shine
Like a jewel polished well,
Hard and clear and fine;
Then soft lilac–and again
On another day
Glimpsed it through a veil of rain,
Shifting, drifting grey.

When the livid waters flee,
Flinching from the storm,
From my window I can see,
Standing safe and warm,
How the white foam tosses high
On the naked shore,
And the breakers' thunder grows
To a battle-roar ...

Far and far I look–Ten miles?
No, for yesterday
Sure I saw the Blessed Isles
Twenty worlds away.
My blue moon of open sea,
Is it little worth?
At the least it gives to me
Keys of all the earth!

Dorothea Mackellar
(1885–1968)

The Tuft of Kelp

All dripping in tangles green,
    Cast up by a lonely sea,
If purer for that, O Weed,
    Bitterer, too, are ye?

Herman Melville
(1819–1891)

The Hidden Tide

Within the world a second world
 That circles ceaselessly:
Stars in the sky and sister stars–
 Turn in your eyes and see!

Tides of the sea that rise and fall
 Aheave from Pole to Pole–
And kindred swayings, veiled but felt,
 That noise along the soul.

You moon, noon-rich, high-throned, remote,
 And pale with pride extreme,
Draws up the sea, but what white moon
 Exalts the tide of Dream?

The Fisher-Folk who cast their nets
 In vision's golden tide
Oft brings to light misshapen shells,
 And nothing worth beside.

And so their worn hands droop adown,
 Their singing throats are dumb;
The Inner-Deep withholds its pearls
 Till turn of tide be come.

But patience! wait—the good tide turns,
  The water's inward set;
And lo, behold! aleap, alive
  With glowing fish the net!

O Toilers of the Hidden Seas!
  Ye have strange gain and loss,
Dragging the Deeps of Soul for pearls,
  And oftimes netting dross.

Flushed to the lips with golden light,
  And dark with sable gloom;
Thrilled by a thousand melodies,
  And silent like a tomb.

Fierce are the winds across your realm,
  As though some Demon veiled
Had loosed the gales of Spirit-land
  To ravage ways unsailed.

But still sweet hours befall at times,
  Rich-lit and full of ease;
The afterglow is like the light
  Of sunset on tired seas.

And worse, perhaps, may be the lot
  Of those whose fate is sleep;
The sodden souls without a tide,
  Dense as a rotten deep.

Pain paves the way for keener joy,
  And wondrous thoughts uproll
When the large moon of Peace looks down
  On high tide in the soul.

Roderic Quinn
(1867–1949)

Sea-Grief

Along the serried coast the Southerly raves,
   Grey birds scream landward through the distance hoar,
   And, swinging from the dim confounded shore,
The everlasting boom of broken waves.

Like muffled thunder rolls about the graves
   Of all the wonder-lands and lives of yore,
   Whose bones asunder bleach for evermore,
In sobbing chasms and under choking caves.

O breaking heart—whose only rest is rage,
   White tossing arms, and lips that kiss and part
   In lonely dreams of love's wild ecstasy.

Not the mean earth thy suffering can assuage
   Nor highest heaven fulfill thy hungry heart,
   O fair full-bosomed passionate weeping sea.

Dowell O'Reilly
(1865–1923)

Shiver Me Timbers!

Dirge from *The Tempest*

Full fadom five thy Father lies,
Of his bones are Corrall made:
Those are pearl's that were his eyes,
Nothing of him that doth fade,
But doth suffer a Sea-change
Into something rich and strange:
Sea-nymphs hourly ring his knell.
Hark now I hear them, ding-dong bell.

William Shakespeare
(1564–1616)

O Captain! my Captain! our fearful trip is done;
The ship has weather'd every rack, the prize we sought is won;
The port is near, the bells I hear, the people all exulting,
While follow eyes the steady keel, the vessel grim and daring:
  But O heart! heart! heart!
    O the bleeding drops of red,
      Where on the deck my Captain lies,
        Fallen cold and dead.

O Captain! my Captain! rise up and hear the bells;
Rise up–for you the flag is flung–for you the bugle trills;
For you bouquets and ribbon'd wreaths–for you the shores
    a-crowding;
For you they call, the swaying mass, their eager faces turning;
  Here Captain! dear father!
    This arm beneath your head;
      It is some dream that on the deck,
        You've fallen cold and dead.

My Captain does not answer, his lips are pale and still;
My father does not feel my arm, he has no pulse nor will;
The ship is anchor'd safe and sound, its voyage closed and done;
From fearful trip, the victor ship, comes in with object won;
  Exult O shores, and ring O bells!
  But I, with mournful tread,
    Walk the deck my Captain lies,
      Fallen cold and dead.

Walt Whitman
(1819–1892)

Under the Surface

On the surface, foam and roar,
    Restless heave and passionate dash,
Shingle rattle along the shore,
    Gathering boom and thundering crash.

Under the surface, soft green light,
    A hush of peace and an endless calm,
Winds and waves from a choral height,
    Falling sweet as a far-off psalm.

On the surface, swell and swirl,
    Tossing weed and drifting waif,
Broken spars that the mad waves whirl,
    Where wreck-watching rocks they chafe.

Under the surface, loveliest forms.
    Feathery fronds with crimson curl,
Treasures too deep for the raid of storms,
    Delicate coral and hidden pearl.

On the surface, lilies white,
    A painted skiff with a singing crew,
Sky-reflections soft and bright,
    Tremulous crimson, gold and blue.

Under the surface, life in death,
    Slimy tangle and oozy moans,
Creeping things with watery breath,
    Blackening roots and whitening bones.

On the surface, a shining reach,
    A crystal couch for the moonbeams' rest,
Starry ripples along the beach,
    Sunset songs from the breezy west.

Under the surface, glooms and fears,
    Treacherous currents swift and strong,
Deafening rush in the drowning ears,–
    Have ye rightly read my song?

Frances Ridley Havergal
(1836–1879)

The City in the Sea

Lo! Death has reared himself a throne
In a strange city lying alone
Far down within the dim West,
Where the good and the bad and the worst and the best
Have gone to their eternal rest.
There shrines and palaces and towers
(Time-eaten towers that tremble not!)
Resemble nothing that is ours.
Around, by lifting winds forgot,
Resignedly beneath the sky
The melancholy waters he.

No rays from the holy heaven come down
On the long night-time of that town;
But light from out the lurid sea
Streams up the turrets silently–
Gleams up the pinnacles far and free
Up domes–up spires–up kingly halls
Up fanes–up Babylon-like walls
Up shadowy long-forgotten bowers
Of sculptured ivy and stone flowers–
Up many and many a marvellous shrine
Whose wreathed friezes intertwine
The viol, the violet, and the vine.
Resignedly beneath the sky
The melancholy waters lie.
So blend the turrets and shadows there
That all seem pendulous in air,
While from a proud tower in the town
 Death looks gigantically down.

There open fanes and gaping graves
Yawn level with the luminous waves;
But not the riches there that lie
In each idol's diamond eye–
Not the gaily-jewelled dead
Tempt the waters from their bed;
For no ripples curl, alas!
Along that wilderness of glass–
No swellings tell that winds may be
Upon some far-off happier sea–
No heavings hint that winds have been
On seas less hideously serene.

But lo, a stir is in the air!
The wave– there is a movement there!
As if the towers had thrust aside,
In slightly sinking, the dull tide–
As if their tops had feebly given
A void within the filmy Heaven.
The waves have now a redder glow–
The hours are breathing faint and low
And when, amid no earthly moans,
Down, down that town shall settle hence,
Hell, rising from a thousand thrones,
Shall do it reverence.

Edgar Allen Poe
(1809–1849)

The Titanic

Forth flashed the serpent streak of steel,
Consummate crown of man's device;
Down crashed upon an immobile
And brainless barrier of ice.
Courage!
The grey gods shoot a laughing lip:-
Let not faith founder with the ship!

We reel before the blows of fate;
Our stout souls stagger at the shock.
Oh! there is Something ultimate
Fixed faster than the living rock.
Courage!
Catastrophe beyond belief
Harden our hearts to fear and grief!

The gods upon the Titans shower
Their high intolerable scorn;
But no god knoweth in what hour
A new Prometheus may be born.
Courage!
Man to his doom goes driving down;
A crown of thorns is still a crown!

No power of nature shall withstand
At last the spirit of mankind:
It is not built upon the sand;
It is not wastrel to the wind.
Courage!
Disaster and destruction tend
To taller triumph in the end.

Aleister Crowley
(1875–1947)

The Sea-Ritual

Prayer unread, and Mass unsung,
Deadman's dirge must still be rung;
  Dingle-dong, the deadbells sound,
  Mermen chant his dirge around!

Wash him bloodless, smoothe him fair,
Stretch his limbs, and sleek his hair:
  Dingle-dong, the deadbells go!
  Mermen swing them to and fro!

In the wormless sand shall he
Feast for no foul gluttons be:
  Dingle-dong, the deadbells chime!
  Mermen keep the tune and time!

We must with a tombstone brave
Shut the shark from out of his grave:
  Dingle-dong, the deadbells toll!
  Mermen ring his requiem-knoll!

Such a slab will we lay o'er him
All the dead shall rise before him!
  Dingle-dong, the deadbells boom!
  Mermen lay him in his tomb!

George Darley
(1795–1846)

The Sea-Queen

The day dies down into deepening gloom, and the wind for once is still,
And the shadows rise in a dim dark pool to the height of the window sill;
The old house creaks as the silence spreads unruffled and vast and drear,
Till the slightest sound is an echoing knell as it falls on the startled ear.

The sand lies glimmering, strange and grey, at the foot of the craggy steep,
While the ominous, inky, sullen sea has lulled its waves to sleep,
And the snags stand gaunt on the desolate shore 'mid the sea-weed dry and stiff,
Where bleaching bones of shipwrecked men show faint at the foot of the cliff.

Alone in the creaking house I sit, and know that the end must be
Some day, by a way that I cannot escape, in this house by the wintry sea;
Where memory broods o'er the days of old as the shapes creep forth and stare,
And the wan white face of my Love looks out from the shadowy mist of her hair.

The wan white face of my Love in pain, who stretches her arms to speak,
And I strive to hear, and listen in vain, as the oaken timbers creak,
Or I catch her footfall soft and light, and turn, but she is not there–
My Love, who sleeps on the couch of Death in the land of my hope's despair.

Oh, why is my heart so sick with dread, and what has my soul to fear,
When the ultimate realm of Death itself keeps all that I hold most dear?
My beautiful Love, with her beautiful hands and her lips with their flagrant
  breath,
Shall press my face to her own once more, yes, there in the land of Death.

Yet still through the creak of the dismal house I hear a pitiful sigh,
And a warning tells me my hope is vain, yet how can I else than die?
A raven sweeps by the window pane from his haunt on the storm-rent hill,
And a log from the fire slips down with a crash; then even the house is still.

And ever the months and the years have gone and ever that low sad sigh
In the weary house by the perilous shore, where my only hope is to die;

And ever the months and the years have gone and ever that low sad sigh
In the weary house by the perilous shore, where my only hope is to die;
And menacing half-seen forms appear remorseless, cruel, and grim,
Whose long lean arms, reaching out as I pass, still lurk in the shadows dim.

And they draw me near to the window pane, where I cannot avoid the sight,
As the moon with her deadly sapphire sheen sheds ever her loveless light;
And I shut my eyes, but my ears must hear whatever the curse may bring,
And, if my resisting eyes unclose, I shall see the fearful thing.

For the doom has come, it is all around, oppressive and near and still,
And I struggle to free myself, close pressed by those arms 'gainst the window sill.
Then sudden I hear the harrowing cry of my Love in her fear for me,
And my limbs grow numb and the cold sweat falls as the terror comes over
    the sea

While a sound, enticing, alluring, wild, wells up from the hideous night,
Of a music that thrills through my quivering nerves with the pain of a fierce
    delight,
And, could I but keep my eyelids closed, who knows but the hour might turn?
Yet my courage fails as the spirit quails, and I open them wide and learn.

And here, below, at the water's marge, there sits in the dreary light
A maiden, shaped for a god to limn, with ivory form and white;
Her locks more dense than the inky deep and her splendid limbs all bare,
While the gleaming glint of her shoulder shows through the wealth of her
    wonderful hair.

And oh, her magical twin white breasts and her delicate, slender throat,
And the mystical curve of the rare red lips whence the ravishing melodies float;
So finely modelled and clearly cut is the scheme of her body's grace–
Oh, how can my spirit dare to endure the enchanting lure of her face?

Yet your eyes are cruel and grey, Sea-Queen, and your lips are too luscious
    and sweet,
As a poisoned flower in the glade that shows its beauty of dark deceit;
And the rippling strength of your agile form is hard, unyielding, and chill:
You could never nestle by me, Sea-Queen, softly and warm and still.

But I feel the spell of your passionate song and am thralled by your witching
    gaze,
And the murky mass of your marvellous hair has twined my heart in its maze,
And your lovely limbs with the pleading arms and your exquisite hands and feet
Are drawing the uttermost deeps of my soul:—You are cruel, in sooth,—but sweet.

And sweet is the thought of your strange embrace; yet what are the bones
    on the shore,
Whose immortal souls have you made your own and whose bodies are seen
    no more?
Oh, why must you take my soul, Sea-Queen; and your kisses, oh, why must
    they be
Dear bought, at so vast a price of doom, on the strand of this wintry sea?

But now you have made me your own, Sea-Queen, and bewildered and thralled
    I go
Where ruby-tipped are the breasts of pearl on that bosom of coldest snow.
Yet oh! as I pass from the haunted house and the threshold of fate is crossed,
I hear the agonised voice of Love that fought for my soul and lost.

And you draw me down with your direful spell in the whirling, narrowing years,
Whose clamouring eddies cannot drown that wild lament in my ears;
And, or ever I touch those frozen lips, I learn at the last, too late,
When clasped in the ice of a dead desire, how this is not love—but hate.

Ian B. Stoughton Holbourn
(1872–1935)

The Rime of the Ancient Mariner

Part I

It is an ancient Mariner,
And he stoppeth one of three.
"By thy long gray beard and glittering eye,
Now wherefore stopp'st thou me?

The Bridegroom's doors are opened wide,
And I am next of kin;
The guests are met, the feast is set:
Mayst hear the merry din."

He holds him with his skinny hand;
"There was a ship," quoth he.
"Hold off! unhand me, graybeard loon!"
Eftsoons his hand dropt he.

He holds him with his glittering eye–
The Wedding-Guest stood still,
And listens like a three-years' child:
The Mariner hath his will.

The Wedding-Guest sat on a stone:
He cannot choose but hear;
And thus spake on that ancient man,
The bright-eyed Mariner:

"The ship was cheered, the harbour cleared,
Merrily did we drop
Below the kirk, below the hill,
Below the lighthouse top.

The Sun came up upon the left,
Out of the sea came he;
And he shone bright, and on the right
Went down into the sea.

Higher and higher every day,
Till over the mast at noon"–
The Wedding-Guest here beat his breast,
For he heard the loud bassoon.

The bride hath paced into the hall,
Red as a rose is she:
Nodding their heads, before her goes
The merry minstrelsy.

The Wedding-Guest he beat his breast,
Yet he cannot choose but hear!
And thus spake on that ancient man,
The bright-eyed Mariner:

"And now the storm-blast came, and he
Was tyrannous and strong;
He struck with his o'ertaking wings,
And chased us south along.

With sloping masts, and dipping prow,
As who pursued with yell and blow
Still treads the shadow of his foe,
And forward bends his head;
The ship drove fast, loud roared the blast,
And southward aye we fled.

And now there came both mist and snow,
And it grew wondrous cold;
And ice mast-high came floating by,
As green as emerald.

And through the drifts, the snowy clifts
Did send a dismal sheen:
Nor shapes of men nor beasts we ken–
The ice was all between.

The ice was here, the ice was there,
The ice was all around;
It cracked and growled, and roared and howled,
Like noises in a swound!

At length did cross an Albatross,
Thorough the fog it came;
As if it had been a Christian soul,
We hailed it in God's name.

It ate the food it ne'er had eat,
And round and round it flew;
The ice did split with a thunder-fit;
The helmsman steered us through!

And a good south wind sprung up behind;
The Albatross did follow,
And every day, for food or play,
Came to the mariner's hollo!

In mist or cloud, on mast or shroud
It perched for vespers nine;
While all the night, through fog-smoke white,
Glimmered the white Moon-shine."

"God save thee, ancient Mariner,
From the fiends that plague thee thus!
Why look'st thou so?"—With my cross-bow
I shot the Albatross.

Part II
The Sun now rose upon the right;
Out of the sea came he,
Still hid in mist, and on the left
Went down into the sea.

And the good south wind still blew behind,
But no sweet bird did follow,
Nor any day, for food or play,
Came to the mariners' hollo!

And I had done a hellish thing,
And it would work 'em woe;
For all averred, I had killed the bird
That made the breeze to blow.
"Ah, wretch!" said they, "the bird to slay
That mad the breeze to blow!"

Nor dim nor red, like God's own head,
The glorious sun uprist;
Then all averred, I had killed the bird
That brought the fog and mist.
"'Twas right," said they, "such birds to slay
That bring the fog and mist."

The fair breeze blew, the white foam flew,
The furrow followed free;
We were the first that ever burst
Into that silent sea.

Down dropt the breeze, the sails dropt down,
'Twas sad as sad could be;
And we did speak only to break
The silence of the sea!

All in a hot and copper sky,
The bloody Sun, at noon,
Right up above the mast did stand,
No bigger than the Moon.

Day after day, day after day,
We stuck, nor breath nor motion;
As idle as a painted ship
Upon a painted ocean.

Water, water everywhere,
And all the boards did shrink,
Water, water everywhere,
Nor any drop to drink.

The very deep did rot: O Christ!
That ever this should be!
Yea, slimy things did crawl with legs
Upon the slimy sea.

About, about, in reel and rout,
The death-fires danced at night;
The water, like a witch's oils,
Burnt green, and blue, and white.

And some in dreams assured were
Of the spirit that plagued us so;
Nine fathom deep he had followed us
From the land of mist and snow.

And every tongue, through utter drought,
Was withered at the root:
We could not speak, no more than if
We had been choked with soot.

Ah, well-a-day! what evil looks
Had I from old and young!
Instead of the cross, the Albatross
About my neck was hung.

Part III
"There passed a weary time. Each throat
Was parched, and glazed each eye.
A weary time! A weary time!
How glazed each weary eye!
When looking westward, I beheld
A something in the sky.

At first it seemed a little speck,
And then it seemed a mist;
It moved, and moved, and took at last
A certain shape, I wist.

A speck, a mist, a shape, I wist!
And still it neared and neared:
As if it dodged a water-sprite,
It plunged, and tacked, and veered.

With throats unslaked, with black lips baked,
We could nor laugh nor wail;
Through utter drought all dumb we stood;
I bit my arm, I sucked the blood,
And cried: "A sail! A sail!""

With throats unslaked, with black lips baked,
Agape they heard me call;
Gramercy! they for joy did grin,
And all at once their breath drew in,
As they were drinking all.

"See! see!" I cried; "she tacks no more!
Hither to work us weal,
Without a breeze, without a tide,
She steadies with upright keel!"

The western wave was all aflame,
The day was well-nigh done,
Almost upon the western wave
Rested the broad bright Sun;
When that strange shape drove suddenly
Betwixt us and the Sun.

And straight the Sun was flecked with bars,
(Heaven's mother send us grace!)
As if through a dungeon grate he peered
With broad and burning face.

"Alas!" thought I, and my heart beat loud,
"How fast she nears and nears!
Are those her sails that glance in the Sun,
Like restless gossameres?

Are those her ribs through which the Sun
Did peer, as through a grate?
And is that Woman all her crew?
Is that a Death? and are there two?
Is Death that Woman's mate?

Her lips were red, her looks were free,
Her locks were yellow as gold:
Her skin was as white as leprosy,
The Nightmare Life-in-Death was she,
Who thicks man's blood with cold.

The naked hulk alongside came,
And the twain were casting dice;
"The game is done! I've won! I've won!"
Quoth she, and whistles thrice.

The Sun's rim dips; the stars rush out:
At one stride comes the dark;
With far-heard whisper, o'er the sea,
Off shot the spectre-bark.

We listened and looked sideways up!
Fear at my heart, as at a cup,
My life-blood seemed to sip!
The stars were dim, and thick the night,
The steersman's face by his lamp gleamed white;
From the sails the dew did drip–
Till clomb above the eastern bar
The hornèd Moon, with one bright star
Within the nether tip.

One after one, by the star-dogged Moon,
Too quick for groan or sigh,
Each turned his face with a ghastly pang,
And cursed me with his eye.

Four times fifty living men
(And I heard nor sigh nor groan),
With heavy thump, a lifeless lump,
They dropt down one by one.

The souls did from their bodies fly—
They fled to bliss or woe!
And every soul it passed me by
Like the whizz of my cross-bow!

Part IV
"I fear thee, ancient Mariner;
I fear thy skinny hand!
And thou art long, and lank, and brown,
As is the ribbed sea-sand.

I fear thee and thy glittering eye,
And thy skinny hand, so brown."—
'Fear not, fear not, thou Wedding-Guest,
This body dropt not down.

Alone, alone, all, all alone,
Alone on a wide, wide sea!
And never a saint took pity on
My soul in agony.

The many men so beautiful!
And they all dead did lie;
And a thousand thousand slimy things
Lived on: and so did I.

I looked upon the rotting sea,
And drew my eyes away:
I looked upon the rotting deck,
And there the dead men lay.

I looked to the heavens, and tried to pray;
But or ever a prayer had gushed,
A wicked whisper came and made
My heart as dry as dust.

I closed my lids, and kept them close,
And the balls like pulses beat;
For the sky and the sea, and the sea and the sky,
Lay like a load on my weary eye,
And the dead were at my feet.

The cold sweat melted from their limbs,
Nor rot nor reek did they;
The look with which they looked on me
Had never passed away.

An orphan's curse would drag to hell
A spirit from on high;
But oh! more horrible than that
Is the curse in a dead man's eye!
Seven days, seven nights, I saw that curse—
And yet I could not die.

The moving Moon went up the sky,
And nowhere did abide;
Softly she was going up,
And a star or two beside.

Her beams bemocked the sultry main,
Like April hoar-frost spread;
But where the ship's huge shadow lay,
The charmèd water burned alway
A still and awful red.

Beyond the shadow of the ship
I watched the water-snakes:
They moved in tracks of shining white,
And when they reared, the elfish light
Fell off in hoary flakes.

Within the shadow of the ship
I watched their rich attire;
Blue, glossy green, and velvet black,
They coiled and swam; and every track
Was a flash of golden fire.

O happy living things! no tongue
Their beauty might declare:
A spring of love gushed from my heart,
And I blest them unaware:
Sure my kind saint took pity on me,
And I blest them unaware.

The self-same moment I could pray;
And from my neck so free
TheAalbatross fell off, and sank
Like lead into the sea.

Part V
"O sleep! it is a gentle thing,
Beloved from pole to pole!
To Mary Queen the praise by given!
She sent the gentle sleep from Heaven,
That slid into my soul.

The silly buckets on the deck
That had so long remained,
I dreamt that they were filled with dew,
And when I woke, it rained.

My lips were wet, my throat was cold,
My garments all were dank;
Sure I had drunken in my dreams,
And still my body drank.

I moved, and could not feel my limbs:
I was so light–almost
I thought that I had died in sleep,
And was a blesséd ghost.

And soon I heard a roaring wind;
It did not come anear;
But with its sound it shook the sails
That were so thin and sere.

The upper air burst into life!
And a hundred fire-flags sheen;
To and fro they were hurried about!
And to and fro, and in and out,
The wan stars danced between.

And the coming wind did roar more loud,
And the sails did sigh like sedge;
And the rain poured down from one black cloud;
The Moon was at its edge.

The thick black cloud was cleft, and still
The Moon was at its side;
Like waters shot from some high crag,
The lightning fell with never a jag,
A river steep and wide.

The loud wind never reached the ship,
Yet now the ship moved on!
Beneath the lightning and the Moon
The dead men gave me a groan.

They groaned, they stirred, they all uprose,
Nor spake, nor moved their eyes;
It had been strange, even in a dream,
To have seen those dead men rise.

The helmsman steered, the ship moved on,
Yet never a breeze upblew;
The mariners all 'gan work the ropes
Where they were wont to do;
They raised their limbs like lifeless fools–
We were a ghastly crew.

The body of my brother's son
Stood by me knee to knee:
The body and I pulled at one rope,
But he said naught to me."

"I fear thee, ancient Mariner!'
"Be calm, thou Wedding-Guest,
"Twas not those souls that fled in pain,
Which to their corses came again,
But a troop of spirits blest:

For when it dawned–they dropped their arms,
And clustered round the mast;
Sweet sounds rose slowly through their mouths,
And from their bodies passed.

Around, around, flew each sweet sound,
Then darted to the Sun;
Slowly the sounds came back again,
Now mixed, now one by one.

Sometimes a-dropping from the sky
I heard the skylark sing;
Sometimes all little birds that are,
How they seemed to fill the sea and air,
With their sweet jargoning!

And now 'twas like all instruments;
Now like a lonely flute,

And now it is an angel's song,
That makes the heavens be mute.

It ceased: yet still the sails made on
A pleasant noise till noon,
A noise like of a hidden brook
In the leafy month of June,
That to the sleeping woods all night
Singeth a quiet tune.

Till noon we quietly sailèd on,
Yet never a breeze did breathe:
Slowly and smoothly went the ship,
Moved onward from beneath.

Under the keel nine fathom deep,
From the land of mist and snow,
The spirit slid; and it was he
That made the ship to go.
The sails at noon left off their tune,
And the ship stood still also.

The Sun, right up above the mast,
Had fixed her to the ocean;
But in a minute she 'gan stir
With a short uneasy motion–
Backwards and forwards half her length,
With a short uneasy motion.

Then like a pawing horse let go,
She made a sudden bound;
It flung the blood into my head,
And I fell down in a swound.

How long in that same fit I lay,
I have not to declare;

But ere my living life returned,
I heard, and in my soul discerned,
Two voices in the air.

"Is it he?" quoth one; "is this the man?
By Him who died on cross,
With his cruel bow he laid full low
The harmless Albatross.

The Spirit who bideth by himself
In the land of mist and snow,
He loved the bird that loved the man
Who shot him with his bow."

The other was a softer voice,
As soft as honey-dew;
Quoth he: "The man hath penance done,
And penance more will do."

Part VI
First Voice:
"But tell me, tell me, speak again,
Thy soft response renewing–
What makes that ship drive on so fast?
What is the Ocean doing?"

Second Voice:
"Still as a slave before his lord,
The Ocean hath no blast;
His great bright eye most silently
Up to the Moon is cast–

If he may know which way to go,
For she guides him smooth or grim.
See, brother, see! how graciously
She looketh down on him."

First Voice:
"But why drives on that ship so fast,
Without or wave or wind?"

Second Voice:
"The air is cut away before,
And closes from behind.
Fly, brother, fly! more high, more high,
Or we shall be belated:
For slow and slow that ship will go,
When the Mariner's trance is abated."

I woke, and we were sailing on,
As in a gentle weather:
'Twas night, calm night, the moon was high;
The dead men stood together.

All stood together on the deck,
For a charnel-dungeon fitter:
All fixed on me their stony eyes,
That in the Moon did glitter.

The pang, the curse with which they died,
Had never passed away:
I could not draw my eyes from theirs,
Nor turn them up to pray.

And now this spell was snapt: once more
I viewed the ocean green,
And looked far forth, yet little saw
Of what had else been seen—

Like one that on a lonesome road
Doth walk in fear and dread,
And having once turned round, walks on,
And turns no more his head;

Because he knows a frightful fiend
Doth close behind him tread.

But soon there breathed a wind on me,
Nor sound nor motion made;
Its path was not upon the sea,
In ripple or in shade.

It raised my hair, it fanned my cheek
Like a meadow-gale of spring–
It mingled strangely with my fears,
Yet it felt like a welcoming.

Swiftly, swiftly flew the ship,
Yet she sailed softly too;
Sweetly, sweetly blew the breeze–
On me alone it blew.

Oh, dream of joy! is this indeed
The lighthouse top I see?
Is this the hill? is this the kirk?
Is this mine own countree?

We drifted o'er the harbour-bar,
And I with sobs did pray–
"O let me be awake, my God,
Or let me sleep alway!"

The harbour-bay was clear as glass,
So smoothly it was strewn!
And on the bay the moonlight lay,
And the shadow of the Moon.

The rock shone bright, the kirk no less,
That stands above the rock;
The moonlight steeped in silentness,
The steady weathercock.

And the bay was white with silent light,
Till rising from the same,
Full many shapes that shadows were,
In crimson colours came.

A little distance from the prow
Those crimson shadows were:
I turned my eyes upon the deck—
O Christ! what saw I there!

Each corse lay flat, lifeless and flat,
And by the holy rood!
A man all light, a seraph-man,
On every corse there stood!

This seraph-band each waved his hand,
It was a heavenly sight!
They stood as signals to the land,
Each one a lovely light;

This seraph-band each waved his hand,
No voice did they impart—
No voice; but oh! the silence sunk
Like music on my heart.

But soon I heard the dash of oars,
I heard the Pilot's cheer;
My head was turned perforce away,
And I saw a boat appear.

The Pilot and the Pilot's boy,
I heard them coming fast;
Dear Lord in Heaven! it was a joy
The dead mean could not blast.

I saw a third—I heard his voice;
It is the Hermit good;
He singeth loud his godly hymns
That he makes in the wood;
He'll shrieve my soul, he'll wash away
The Albatross's blood.

Part VII
"This Hermit good lives in the wood
Which slopes down to the sea.
How loudly his sweet voice he rears!
He loves to talk with marineres
That come from a far countree.

He kneels at morn, and noon, and eve—
He hath a cushion plump;
It is the moss that wholly hides
The rotted old oak stump.

The skiff-boat neared: I heard them talk,
"Why, this is strange, I trow!
Where are those lights so many and fair
That signal made but now?"

"Strange, by my faith," the Hermit said—
"And they answered not our cheer!
The planks look warped; and see those sails,
How thin they are and sere!
I never saw aught like to them,
Unless perchance it were

Brown skeletons of leaves that lag
My forest-brook along;
When the ivy-tod is heavy with snow,
And the owlet whoops to the wolf below,
That eats the she-wolf's young."

"Dear Lord! it hath a fiendish look,"
The Pilot made reply—
"I am afeared."—"Push on, push on!"
Said the Hermit cheerily.

The boat came closer to the ship,
But I nor spake nor stirred;
The boat came close beneath the ship,
And straight a sound was heard.

Under the water it rumbled on,
Still louder and more dread:
It reached the ship, it split the bay;
The ship went down like lead.

Stunned by that loud and dreadful sound,
Which sky and ocean smote,
Like one that hath been seven days drowned
My body lay afloat;
But swift as dreams, myself I found
Within the Pilot's boat.

Upon the whirl, where sank the ship,
The boat spun round and round;
And all was still, save that the hill
Was telling of the sound.

I moved my lips—the Pilot shrieked,
And fell down in a fit;
The holy Hermit raised his eyes,
And prayed where he did sit.

I took the oars: the Pilot's boy,
Who now doth crazy go,
Laughed loud and long, and all the while
His eyes went to and fro:

"Ha! ha!" quoth he, "full plain I see
The Devil knows how to row!"

And now, all in my own countree,
I stood on the firm land!
The Hermit stepped forth from the boat,
And scarcely he could stand.

"O shrieve me, shrieve me, holy man!"
The hermit crossed his brow:
"Say quick," quoth he, "I bid thee say–
What manner of man art thou?"

Forthwith this frame of mine was wrenched
With a woeful agony,
Which forced me to begin my tale;
And then it left me free.

Since then, at an uncertain hour,
That agony returns;
And till my ghastly tale is told,
This heart within me burns.

I pass, like night, from land to land:
I have strange powers of speech;
That moment that his face I see,
I know the man that must hear me:
To him my tale I teach.

What loud uproar bursts from that door!
The wedding-guests are there:
But in the garden bower the bride
And bridesmaids singing are:
And hark the little versper-bell,
Which biddeth me to prayer!

O Wedding-Guest! this soul hath been
Alone on a wide, wide sea;
So lonely 'twas, that God Himself
Scarce seeméd there to be.

O sweeter than the marriage-feast,
'Tis sweeter far to me,
To walk together to the kirk
With a goodly company! –

To walk together to the kirk,
And all together pray,
While each to his great Father bends,
Old men and babes, and loving friends,
And youths and maidens gay!

Farewell, farewell! but this I tell
To thee, thou Wedding-Guest!
He prayeth well, who loveth well
Both man and bird and beast.

He prayeth best, who loveth best
All things both great and small;
For the dear God who loveth us,
He made and loveth all."

The Mariner, whose eye is bright,
Whose beard with age is hoar,
Is gone; and now the Wedding-Guest
Turned from the bridegroom's door.

He went like one that hath been stunned,
And is of sense forlorn:
A sadder and wiser man
He rose the morrow morn.

Samuel Taylor Coleridge
(1772–1834)

The Sands of Dee

"O Mary, go and call the cattle home,
        And call the cattle home,
        And call the cattle home,
        Across the sands of Dee."
The western wind was wild and dark with foam,
        And all alone went she.

The western tide crept up along the sand,
        And o'er and o'er the sand,
        And round and round the sand,
        As far as the eye could see.
The rolling mist came down and hid the land:
        And never home came she.
"O is it weed, or fish, or floating hair—
        A tress of golden hair
        A drownèd maiden's hair,
        Above the nets at sea?
Was never salmon yet shone so fair
    Among the stakes of Dee."

They row'd her in across the rolling foam,
        The cruel crawling foam,
        The cruel hungry foam,
        To her grave beside the sea.
But still the boatmen hear her call the cattle home,
        Across the sands of Dee.

Charles Kingsley
(1819–1875)

The Fog Siren

The grey mist veils the deep, the seeming ghost,
  Forlorn and olden, of the world's lost seas.
  Veering to fancies of the muffled breeze,
There moans with ocean down the shrouded coast
(Ceaseless, as from the eternal pain and post,
  And born of woe no mortal may appease)
  The siren's grieving, that, as daylight flees,
Summons the drowned, a solemn shadow-host.

Then, as the pallid spectres landward creep,
  Apocalyptic voices haunt the gloom;
We hear, upon the troubling of the deep,
  The bellow of the Beast drawn down to doom;
And rending all Death's empire in its sweep,
  The trumpet's groaning rolls athwart the tomb.

George Sterling
(1869–1926)

The Mariner

Soft came the breath of spring; smooth flow'd the tide;
And blue the heaven in its mirror smil'd;
The white sail trembled, swell'd, expanded wide,
The busy sailors at the anchor toil'd.

With anxious friends, that shed the parting tear,
The deck was throng'd—how swift the moments fly!
The vessel heaves, the farewell signs appear;
Mute is each tongue, and eloquent each eye!

The last dread moment comes!—The sailor-youth
Hides the big drop, then smiles amid his pain,
Soothes his sad bride, and vows eternal truth,
'Farewell, my love—we shall—shall meet again!'

Long on the stern, with waving hand, he stood;
The crowded shore sinks, lessening from his view,
As gradual glides the bark along the flood;
His bride is seen no more—"Adieu!—adieu!"

The breeze of Eve moans low, her smile is o'er,
Dim steals her twilight down the crimson'd west,
He climbs the top-most mast, to seek once more
The far-seen coast, where all his wishes rest.

He views its dark line on the distant sky,
And Fancy leads him to his little home,
He sees his weeping love, he hears her sigh,
He soothes her griefs, and tells of joys to come.

Eve yields to night, the breeze to wintry gales,
In one vast shade the seas and the shore repose;
He turns his aching eyes,—his spirit fails,
The chill tear falls;—sad to the deck he goes!

The storm of midnight swells, the sails are furl'd,
Deep sounds the lead, but finds no friendly shore,
Fast o'er the waves the wretched bark is hurl'd,
"O Ellen, Ellen!' we must meet no more!"

Lightnings, the shew the vast and foamy deep,
The rending thunders, as they onward roll
The loud, loud winds, that o'er the bilows sweep–
Shake the firm nerve, appall the bravest soul!

Ah! what avails the seaman's toiling care!
The straining cordage bursts, the mast is riv'n;
The sounds of terror groan along the air,
Then sink afar;–the bark on rocks is driv'n!

Fierce o'er the wreck the whelming waters pass'd,
The helpless crew sunk in the roaring main!
Henry's faint accents trembled in the blast–
"Farewell, my love!–we ne'er shall meet again!"

Oft, at the calm and silent evening hour,
When summer breezes linger on the wave,
A melancholy voice is heard to pour
Its lonely sweetness o'er poor Henry's grave!

And oft, at midnight, airy strains are heard
Around the grove, where Ellen's form is laid;
Nor is the dirge by village-maidens fear'd,
For lovers' spirits guard the holy shade!

Ann Radcliffe
(1764–1823)

Silberhorn

In Dennis O'Halloran's bar-room, down by Newcastle pier,
(Was ever ye down to Newcastle, lad?), I was sittin' drinkin' a beer,
An' treatin' a girl called Topsy (ye know the kind she'd be),
When somebody called from the doorway, "The *Silberhorn's* going to sea!"

An' I rose from my feet to see her, an' Topsy I pushed aside,
For ye'll see no ship like the *Silberhorn* go out wi' every tide;
An' I stood at the street-side starin' to see the grand packet go by,
Wi' the sunset bright on her beauty, an' her ensign flutterin' high.

I saw John Warren, her skipper, wi' his eyes o' windy grey,
An' her first mate, Willie Dougal, an' her second mate, Tom O'Shay,
An' eight young bonny apprentice boys wavin' the girls farewell,
An' deep from the break of her fo'c'sle came the clang of her big iron bell.

As her bells broke out while she passed me a something gripped my breath,
As slow from her pier she glided, wi' the evenin' still as death;
The sun went under a cloud-bank, an' the dusk came droppin' down,
An' the only sound was the laughter o' the girls o' Newcastle town.

They lowered the grand ship's ensign, an' she slipped away to the night,
Till all I could see in the darkness was the gleam of her binnacle light;
As the girls turned back to the bar-room clear over the steam there came
The long, high echoing sing-song of her chanteyman's refrain.

"Good-bye, fare you well," I heard it, an' a cheer an' an order loud,
As a lone star winked in the darkness from the rim of a driftin' cloud;
An' I called to Dennis O'Halloran to bring me a bottle o' beer,
An' I drank in the bar-room doorway to the ship gone out from her pier.

O'Halloran's rang wi' laughter, but chilly there came o'er me
A feel like the feel o' the midnight when there's drift ice on the sea;
An' the fiddler started fiddlin'; an' Topsy tossed her head:
"You buys me no drink, nor dances? You acts like a man what's dead!"

So I called for a bottle for Topsy, an' forgot the sailor's way,
An' never gave thought to the *Silberhorn* for many an' many a day;
But when next I heard her mentioned I remembered the Newcastle pier
An' the night when I'd drunk to her hearties in a bottle o' Newcastle beer.

"Lost with all hands," I read it; "Lost with all hands." No more;
Never a word o' the latitude, how far or how near the shore;
"Good-bye, fare you well," came ringin', an' a cheer, an' an order high,
From the grand fine packet that evenin' goin' out to the sea to die!

Bill Adams
(1879–1953)

Van Diemen's Land

Clipper ship, clipper ship, sailin' south so fast
Clipper ship, clipper ship, sailin' for southern sand
I don't know what ship he's on
Sailin' south unto Van Diemen's Land.

He don't know what he's headin' for
Down in that south sea convict colony
Moonlight poachers the law does not ignore
Now he's bound for Tasmanian sea.

Clipper ship, clipper ship, sailin' south so fast
Clipper ship, clipper ship, sailin' for southern sand
I don't know what ship he's on
Sailin' south unto Van Diemen's Land.

He rambled free without a care
The law to him was no command
Now he's sailin' fast through the salty air
Sailin' south unto Van Diemen's Land.

When he dies, he won't be in paradise
That convict colony will make him weep
In Tasmanian seas he'll close his eyes
In Van Diemen's Land is where he'll sleep.

Clipper ship, clipper ship, sailin' south so fast
Clipper ship, clipper ship, sailin' for southern sand
I don't know what ship he's on
Sailin' south unto Van Diemen's Land
But I know it's the last ship he's on
Sailin' south unto Van Diemen's Land.

Anon.

Beach Burial

Softly and humbly to the Gulf of Arabs
The convoys of dead sailors come;
At night they sway and wander in the waters far under
But morning rolls them in the foam.

Between the sob and clubbing of the gunfire
Someone, it seems, has time for this,
To pluck them from the shallows and bury them in burrows
And tread the sand upon their nakedness;

And each cross, the driven stake of tidewood,
Bears the last signature of men,
Written with such perplexity, with such bewildered pity,
The words choke as they begin–

'*Unknown seaman*'–the ghostly pencil
Wavers and fades, the purple drips,
The breath of wet season has washed their inscriptions
As blue as drowned men's lips,

Dead seamen, gone in search of the same landfall,
Whether as enemies they fought,
Or fought with us, or neither; the sand joins them together,
Enlisted on the other front.

Kenneth Slessor
(1901–1971)

Stars in the Sea

I took a boat on a starry night
   And went for a row on the water,
And she danced like a child on a wake of light
   And bowed where the ripples caught her.

I vowed, as I rowed on the velvet blue
   Through the night and starry splendour,
To woo and sue a maiden I knew
   Till she bent to my pleadings tender.

My painted boat she was light and glad
   And gladder my heart was wishing,
And I came in time to a little lad
   Who stood on the rocks a-fishing.

I said "Ahoy!" and he said "Ahoy!"
   And I asked how the fish were biting:
"And what are you trying to catch, my boy,
   Bream, silver and red–or whiting?

"Neither," he answered, "the seaweed mars
   My line, and the sharp shells sunder:
I am trying my luck with those great big stars
   Down there in the round skies under.

"Good-bye!" from him, and "Good-bye!" from me,
   And never a laugh came after;
So many go fishing for stars in the sea
   That it's hardly a subject for laughter.

Roderic Quinn
(1867–1949)

Australia

Last sea-thing dredged by sailor Time from Space,
Are you a drift Sargasso, where the West
In halcyon calm rebuilds her fatal nest?
Or Delos of a coming Sun-God's race?
Are you for Light, and trimmed, with oil in place,
Or but a Will o' Wisp on marshy quest?
A new demesne for Mammon to infest?
Or lurks millennial Eden 'neath your face?

The cenotaphs of species dead elsewhere
That in your limits leap and swim and fly,
Or trail uncanny harp-strings from your trees,
Mix omens with the auguries that dare
To plant the Cross upon your forehead sky,
A virgin helpmate Ocean at your knees.

Bernard O'Dowd
(1866–1952)

Ultima Thule

The tides roll white and pale
  On a shingly, stormy strand,
And the seabirds sweep and wail
In the swing of the seaborn gale
      Over the sand,
In Thule, Ultima Thule,
      The lonely land.

Sometimes the icepack white
  Sails by, all silent and grand,
And sometimes the lightning bright
Pierces the heart of the night
      Like a fiery brand,
In Thule, Ultima Thule,
      The lonely land.

Fronting the waters grey,
    The halls of the ancients stand,
Fallen and gone to decay
With those who dwelt on a day,
            A valiant band,
In Thule, Ultima Thule,
            The lonely land.

Once they were kings on the sea;
    Their ships now rot on the sand,
Fall'n is their high roof-tree,
And the fox and the wolf roam free
            In those ruins grand,
In Thule, Ultima Thule,
            The lonely land.

Cicely Fox Smith
(1882–1954)

Flotsam
and Jetsam

The Uses of Ocean

To people who allege that we
Incline to overrate the Sea
I answer, "We do not;
Apart from being colored blue,
It has its uses not a few;
I cannot think what we should do
If ever 'the deep did rot.'"

Take ships, for instance. You will note
That, lacking stuff on which to float,
They could not get about;
Dreadnought and liner, smack and yawl,
And other types that you'll recall–
They simply could not sail at all
If Ocean once gave out.

And see the trouble which it saves
To islands; but for all those waves
That made us what we are—
But for their help so kindly lent,
Europe could march right through to Kent
And never need to circumvent
A single British tar.

Take fish, again. I have in mind
No better field that they could find
For exercise or sport;
How would the whale, I want to know,
The blubbery whale contrive to blow?
Where would your playful kipper go
If the supply ran short?

And hence we rank the Ocean high;
But there are privy reasons why
Its praise is on my lip:
I deem it, when my heart is set
On walking into something wet,
The nicest medium I have met
In which to take a dip.

Sir Owen Seaman
(1861–1936)

The Beach Comber

I'd like to return to the world again,
To the dutiful, work-a-day world of men,–
For I'm sick of the beach-comber's lot,
Of the one volcano flaming hot,
With the snow round its edge and the fire in its throat,
And the tropical island that seems a-float
Like a world set in space all alone in the sea ...
How I wish that a ship, it would stop for me.
I'm sick of the brown girl that loves me, I'm sick
Of the cocoanut groves,–you can't take me too quick
From this place, though it's rich in all nature can give ...
For I want to return where it's harder to live,
Where men struggle for life, where they work and find sweet
Their rest after toil, and the food that they eat ...
What? A ship's in the offing? ... dear God, let me hide,–
They're in need of a sailor, are waiting for the tide
To put off? ... I will hide where the great cliff hangs sheer–
Give 'em mangoes and goats, and don't tell 'em I'm here!

Harry Kemp
(1883–1960)

Stately as a Galleon

My neighbour, Mrs Fanshaw, is portly-plump and gay,
She must be over sixty-seven, if she is a day.
You might have thought her life was dull,
It's one long whirl instead.
I asked her about it, and this is what she said:

I've joined an Olde Thyme Dance Club, the trouble is that there
Are too many ladies over, and no gentlemen to spare.
It seems a shame, it's not the same,
But still it has to be,
Some ladies have to dance together,
One of them is me.

Stately as a galleon, I sail across the floor,
Doing the Military Two-step, as in the days of yore.
I dance with Mrs Tiverton; she's light on her feet, in spite
Of turning the scale at fourteen stone, and being of medium height.
So gay the band,
So giddy the sight,
Full evening dress is a must,
But the zest goes out of a beautiful waltz
When you dance it bust to bust.

So, stately as a galleon, I sail across the floor,
Doing the Valse Valeta as in the days of yore.
The gent is Mrs Tiverton, I am her lady fair,
She bows to me ever so nicely and I curtsey to her with care.
So gay the band,
So giddy the sight,
But it's not the same in the end
For a lady is never a gentleman, though
She may be your bosom friend.

So, stately as a galleon, I sail across the floor,
Doing the dear old Lancers, as in the days of yore.
I'm led by Mrs Tiverton, she swings me round and round
And though she manoeuvres me wonderfully well
I never get off the ground.
So gay the band,
So giddy the sight,
I try not to get depressed.
And it's done me a power of good to explode,
And get this off my chest.

Joyce Grenfell
(1910–1979)

Of all the ships upon the blue,
No ship contained a better crew
Than that of worthy CAPTAIN REECE
Commanding of *The Mantelpiece.*

He was adored by all his men,
For worthy CAPTAIN REECE, R.N.,
Did all that lay within him to
Promote the comfort of his crew.

If ever they were dull or sad,
Their captain danced to them like mad,
Or told, to make the time pass,
Droll legends of his infancy.

A feather bed had every man,
Warm slippers and hot-water can,
Brown windsor from the captain's store,
A valet, too, to every four.

Did they with thirst in summer burn?
Lo, seltzogenes at every turn,
And on all very sultry days
Cream ices handed round on trays.

Then currant wine and ginger pops
Stood handily on all the "tops";
And, also with amusement rife,
A "Zoetrope, or Wheel of Life."

New volumes came across the sea,
From MISTER MUDIE'S libraree;
The Times and *Saturday Review*
Beguiled the leisure of the crew.

Kind-hearted CAPTAIN REECE, R.N.,
Was quite devoted to his men;
In point of fact, good CAPTAIN REECE
Beatified *The Mantelpiece.*

One summer eve, at half-past ten,
He said (addressing all his men):
"Come, tell me please, what can I do
To please and gratify my crew?

"By any reasonable plan
I'll make you happy, if I can;
My own convenience count as *nil*;
It is my duty, and I will."

Then up and answered WILLIAM LEE
(The kindly captain's coxswain he,
A nervous, shy, soft-spoken man),
He cleared his throat and thus began:

"You have a daughter, CAPTAIN REECE,
Ten female cousins and a niece,
A ma, if what I'm told is true
Six sisters, and an aunt or two.

"Now, somehow, sir, it seems to me,
More friendly-like we all should be
If you united of 'em to
Unmarried members of the crew.

"If you'd ameliorate our life,
Let each select from them a wife;
And as for nervous me, old pal
Give me your own enchanting gal!'"

Good CAPTAIN REECE, that worthy man,
Debated on his coxswain's plan:
"I quite agree," he said, "O Bill;
It is my duty, and I will.

"My daughter, that enchanting gurl,
Has just been promised to an earl,
And all my other familee,
To peers of various degree.

"But what are dukes and viscounts to
The happiness of all my crew?
The word I gave you I'll fulfil,
It is my duty, and I will."

"As you desire it shall befall,
I'll settle thousands on you all,
And I shall be, despite my hoard,
The only bachelor on board."

The boatswain of *The Mantelpiece*,
He blushed and spoke to CAPTAIN REECE.
"I beg your honour's leave," he said,
"If you would wish to go and wed,

"I have a widowed mother who
Would be the very thing for you
She long has loved you from afar,
She washes for you, CAPTAIN R."

The captain saw the dame that day–
Addressed her in his playful way–
"And did it want a wedding ring?
It was a tempting ickle sing!

"Well, well, the chaplain I will seek,
We'll be married this day week–
At yonder church upon the hill;
It is my duty, and I will!"

The sisters, cousins, aunts and niece,
And widowed ma of CAPTAIN REECE,
Attended there as they were bid;
It was their duty, and they did.

William Schwenck Gilbert
(1836–1911)

The Harbour of Fowey

O the Harbour of Fowey
  Is a beautiful spot,
And it's there I enjowey
  To sail in a yot;
Or to race in a yacht
  Round a mark or a buoy–
Such a beautiful spacht
  Is the Harbour of Fouy!

When her anchor is weighed
  And the water she ploughs,
Upon neat lemoneighed
  O it's then I caroughs;
And I take Watt's hymns
  And I sing them aloud
When it's homeward she skymns
  O'er the waters she ploud.

But the wave-mountain high,
  And the violent storm,
Do I risk them? Not igh!
  But prefer to sit worm
With a book on my knees
  By the library fire,
While I list to the brees
  Rising hire and hire.

And so, whether I weigh
  Up the anchor or not,
I am happy each deigh
  In my home or my yot;
Every care I resign,
  Every comfort enjoy,
In this cottage of mign
  By the Harbour of Foy.

And my leisure's addressed
  To composing of verse
Which, if hardly the bessed,
  Might be easily werse.
And, the spelling I use
  Should the critics condemn,
Why, I have my own vuse
  And I don't think of themn.

Yes, I have my own views:
  But the teachers I follow
Are the Lyrical Miews
  And the Delphic Apollow.
Unto them I am debtor
  For spelling and rhyme,
And I'm doing it bebtor
  And bebtor each rhyme.

Sir Arthur Quiller Couch
(1863–1944)

A South Sea Ballad

In London stands a famous pile,
  And near that pile an Alley,
Where merry crowds for riches toil,
  And wisdom stoops to folly.
Here, sad and joyful, high and low,
  Court Fortune for her graces;
And as she smiles or frowns, they show
  Their gestures and their grimaces.

Here, Stars and Garters do appear
  Among our lords the rabble;
To buy and sell, to see and hear
  The Jews and Gentiles squabble.
Here, crafty Courtiers are too wise
  For those who trust to fortune;
They see the cheat with clearer eyes,
  Who peep behind the curtain.

Long heads may thrive, by sober rules;
  Because they think, and drink not;
But headlongs are our thriving fools,
  Who only drink, and think not.
The lucky rogues like spaniel dogs,
  Leap into South Sea water;
And there they fish for golden frogs,
  Nor caring what comes after.

'Tis said that alchemists of old
  Could turn a brazen kettle,
Or leaden cistern into gold;
  That noble tempting metal.
But (if it here may be allowed,
  To bring in great with small things)
Our cunning South Sea like a god,
  Turns nothing into all things.

What need we of Indian wealth,
  Or commerce with our neighbours;
Our Consitution is in health,
  And riches crown our labours.
Our South Sea ships have golden shrouds,
  They bring us wealth 'tis granted:
But lodge their treasures in the clouds,
  To hide it till it's wanted.

O, Britain! bless thy present state!
  Thou only happy nation!
So oddly rich, so madly great,
  Since Bubbles came in fashion.
Successful rakes exert their pride,
  And count their airy millions;
Whilst homely drabs in coaches ride,
  Brought up to Town on pillions.

Few men who follow reason's rules,
　　Grow fat with South Sea diet;
Young rattles and unthinking fools
　　Are those that flourish by it.
Old musty jades, and pushing blades,
　　Who've least consideration,
Grow rich apace; while wiser heads
　　Are struck with admiration.

A race of men, who, t'other day,
　　Lay crushed beneath disasters,
Are now, by Stock, brought into play,
　　And made our lords and masters.
But should our South Sea Babel fall,
　　What numbers would be frowning;
The losers then must case their gall
　　By hanging, or by drowning.

Five hundred millions, notes and bonds,
　　Our Stocks are worth in value:
But neither lie in goods, or lands,
　　Or money, let me tell ye.
Yet though our foreign trade is lost,
　　Of mighty wealth we vapour;
When all the riches that we boast
　　Consist of scraps of paper.

Ned Ward
(1667–1731)

To a Young Lady, With Some Lampreys

With lovers, 'twas of old the fashion
By presents to convey their passion;
No matter what the gift they sent,
The Lady saw that love was meant.
Fair *Atalanta*, as a favour,
Took the boar's head her Hero gave her;
Nor could the bristly thing affront her,
'Twas a fit present from a hunter.
When Squires send woodcocks to the dame,
It serves to show their absent flame:
Some by a snip of woven hair,
In posied lockets bribe the fair;
How many mercenary matches
Have sprung from Di'mond-rings and watches!
But hold—a ring, a watch, a locket,
Would drain at once a Poet's pocket;
He should send songs that cost him nought,
Nor ev'n he prodigal of thought.
Why then send Lampreys? fye, for shame!
'Twill set a virgin's blood on flame.
This to fifteen a proper gift!
It might lend sixty five a lift.
I know your maiden Aunt will scold,
And think my present somewhat bold.
I see her lift her hands and eyes.

"What eat it, Niece? eat *Spanish* flies!
Lamprey's a most immodest diet:
You'll neither wake nor sleep in quiet.
Should I to night eat Sago cream,
'Twould make me blush to tell my dream;

If I eat Lobster, 'tis so warming,
That ev'ry man I see looks charming;
Wherefore had not the filthy fellow
Laid *Rochester* upon your pillow?
I vow and swear, I think the present
Had been as modest and as decent.
Who has her virtue in her power?
Each day has its unguarded hour;
Always in danger of undoing,
A prawn, a shrimp may prove our ruin!
The shepherdess, who lives on salad,
To cool her youth, controuls her palate;
Should *Dian's* maids turn liqu'rish livers,
And of huge lampreys rob the rivers,
Then all beside each glade and Visto,
You'd see Nymphs lying like *Calisto*.
The man who meant to heat your blood,
Needs not himself such vicious food–"

In this, I own, your Aunt is clear,
I sent you what I well might spare:
For when I see you, (without joking)
Your eyes, lips, breasts, are so provoking,
They set my heart more cock-a-hoop,
Than could whole seas of craw-fish soupe.

John Gay
(1685–1732)

Longfellow's Visit to Venice

(To be read in a quiet New England accent.)

Near the celebrated Lido where the breeze is fresh and free
Stands the ancient port of Venice called the City of the Sea.

All its streets are made of water, all its homes are brick and stone,
Yet it has a picturesqueness which is justly all its own.

Here for centuries have artists come to see the vistas quaint,
Here Bellini set his easel, here he taught his School to paint.

Here the youthful Giorgone gazed upon the domes and towers,
And interpreted his era in a way which pleases ours.

A later artist, Tintoretto, also did his paintings here,
Massive works which generations have continued to revere.

Still to-day come modern artists to portray the buildings fair
And their pictures may be purchased on San Marco's famous Square.

When the bell notes from the belfries and the campaniles chime
Still to-day we find Venetians elegantly killing time

In their gilded old palazzos, while the music in our ears
Is the distant band at Florians mixed with songs of gondoliers.

Thus the New World meets the Old World and the sentiments expressed
Are melodiously mingled in my warm New England breast.

Sir John Betjeman
(1906–1984)

The Walrus and the Carpenter

The sun was shining on the sea,
　Shining with all his might:
He did his very best to make

The billows smooth and bright–
And this was odd, because it was
    The middle of the night.
The moon was shining sulkily,
    Because she thought the sun
Had got no business to be there
    After the day was done–
"It's very rude of him," she said,
    "To come and spoil the fun!"

The sea was wet as wet could be,
    The sands were dry as dry.
You could not see a cloud, because
    No cloud was in the sky:
No birds were flying overhead–
    There were no birds to fly.

The Walrus and the Carpenter
    Were walking close at hand;
They wept like anything to see
    Such quantities of sand:
"If this were only cleared away,"
    They said, "it would be grand!"

"If seven maids with seven mops
    Swept it for half a year.
Do you suppose," the Walrus said,
    "That they could get it clear?"
"I doubt it," said the Carpenter,
    And shed a bitter tear.

"O Oysters, come and walk with us!"
    The Walrus did beseech.
"A pleasant walk, a pleasant talk,
    Along the briny beach:

We cannot do with more than four,
    To give a hand to each."

The eldest Oyster looked at him,
    But never a word he said:
The eldest Oyster winked his eye,
    And shook his heavy head–
Meaning to say he did not choose
    To leave the oyster-bed.
But four young Oysters hurried up,
    All eager for the treat:
Their coats were brushed, their faces washed,
    Their shoes were clean and neat–
And this was odd, because, you know,
    They hadn't any feet.

Four other Oysters followed them,
    And yet another four;
And thick and fast they came at last,
    And more, and more, and more–
All hopping through the frothy waves,
    And scrambling to the shore.

The Walrus and the Carpenter
    Walked on a mile or so,
And then they rested on a rock
    Conveniently low:
And all the little Oysters stood
    And waited in a row.

"The time has come," the Walrus said,
    "To talk of many things:
Of shoes–and ships–and sealing-wax–

Of cabbages—and kings—
And why the sea is boiling hot—
    And whether pigs have wings."

"But wait a bit," the Oysters cried,
    "Before we have our chat;
For some of us are out of breath,
    And all of us are fat!"
"No hurry!" said the Carpenter.
    They thanked him much for that.

"A loaf of bread," the Walrus said,
    "Is what we chiefly need:
Pepper and vinegar besides
    Are very good indeed—
Now if you're ready, Oysters dear,
    We can begin to feed."

"But not on us!" the Oysters cried,
    Turning a little blue.
"After such kindness, that would be
    A dismal thing to do!"
"The night is fine," the Walrus said.
    "Do you admire the view?

"It was so kind of you to come!
    And you are very nice!"
The Carpenter said nothing but
    "Cut us another slice:
I wish you were not quite so deaf—
    I've had to ask you twice!"

"It seems a shame," the Walrus said,
  "To play them such a trick,
After we've brought them out so far,
  And made them trot so quick!"
The Carpenter said nothing but
  "The butter's spread too thick!"

"I weep for you," the Walrus said:
  "I deeply sympathize."
With sobs and tears he sorted out
  Those of the largest size,
Holding his pocket-handkerchief
  Before his streaming eyes.

"O Oysters," said the Carpenter,
  "You've had a pleasant run!
Shall we be trotting home again?"
  But answer came there none–
And this was scarcely odd, because
  They'd eaten every one.

Lewis Carroll
(1832–1898)

Sea Shell

Sea Shell, Sea Shell,
    Sing me a song, O Please!
A song of ships and pirate men,
    And parrots, and tropical trees.

Of islands lost in the Spanish Main
Which no man ever may find again,
Of fishes and corals under the waves,
And sea-horses stabled in great green caves.

Sea Shell, Sea Shell,
Sing of the things you know so well.

Amy Lowell
(1874–1925)

You waves, though you dance by my feet like children at play,
Though you glow and you glance, though you purr and you dart;
In the Junes that were warmer than these are, the waves were more gay,
When I was a boy with never a crack in my heart.

The herring are not in the tides as they were of old;
My sorrow! for many a creak gave the creel in the cart
That carried the take to Sligo town to be sold,
When I was a boy with never a crack in my heart.

And ah, you proud maiden, you are not so fair when his oar
Is heard on the water, as they were, the proud and apart,
Who paced in the eve by the nets on the pebbly shore,
When I was a boy with never a crack in my heart.

William Butler Yeats
(1865–1939)

Index to Poets

Acknowledgements

John Betjeman, 'Longfellow's Visit to Venice', from *Collected Poems* © The Estate of John Betjeman 1955, 1958, 1962, 1964, 1968, 1970, 1979, 1981, 1982, 2001. Reproduced by permission of John Murray (Publishers). Robert P.Tristram Coffin, 'One Who Knows His Sea-gulls' reprinted with kind permission of Macmillan Publishers. Robert Graves, 'Jonah' reprinted with kind permission of Carcanet Press Limited. Joyce Grenfell, 'Stately as a Galleon' from *George, Don't Do That...* by Joyce Grenfell, published by Hodder and Stoughton. Copyright © 1977 Joyce Grenfell. Reproduced by permission of Sheil Land Associates Ltd. Harry Kemp, 'The Beach Comber' reprinted with kind permission of the estate of Harry Kemp. Robert Lowell, 'Dolphin' reprinted with kind permission of Farrar, Straus & Giroux. Dorothy MacKellar, 'The Open Sea' reprinted with kind permission of the estate of Dorothy MacKellar. John Masefield, 'Port of Holy Peter' and 'Sea-Fever' reprinted with kind permission of The Society of Authors. Bernard O'Dowd, 'Australia' reprinted with kind permission of Lothian Books. Edwin John Pratt, 'The Charge of the Swordfish' reprinted with kind permission of the University of Toronto. Roderic Quinn, 'The Hidden Tide' and 'Stars in the Sea' reprinted with kind permission of Angus & Robertson. Edward Shanks, 'Boats at Night' reprinted with kind permission of Macmillan Publishers. Kenneth Slessor, 'Beach Burial' reprinted with kind permission of Angus & Robertson. James Stephens, 'The Shell' reprinted with kind permission of The Society of Authors. Derek Walcott, 'Coral' reprinted with kind permission of the Random House Group Limited. Andrew Young, 'The Chalk-Cliff' reprinted with kind permission of Carcanet Press Limited.

Pavilion Books is committed to respecting the intellectual property rights of others. We have therefore taken all reasonable efforts to ensure that the reproduction of all contents on these pages is done with the full consent of the copyright owners. If you are aware of unintentional omissions, please contact the company directly so that any necessary corrections may be made for future editions.

Picture Credits

Mar y Evans Picture Librar y: p13, p57, p81, p99, p109, p123, p130; Mary Evans Picture Library/ Arthur Rackham: p88; Illustrated London News/ Mary Evans: p19, pp74–75; Interfoto/ Bildarchiv Hansmann/Mary Evans: p104.

NRM Pictorial Collection/Science & Society Picture Library: p 70; Stephen Bone: p176–177; Austin Cooper: p.189; Frank Henry Mason: p34, p92, p182; John MacPherson: p116–117; Ralph Mott: p41; Frank Newbould: p171; Charles Pears: p28, p47; Tom Purvis: p155; Leonard Richmond: p147; Harry Riley: p160; Studio Seven: p61; Herbert Alker Tripp: p52; Norman Wilkinson: p162; National Media Museum/Science & Society Picture Library: p70; Science Museum Library/Science & Society Picture Library: pp84–85.

TfL from the London Transport Museum Collection/Gregory Brown: p9.